TOURIST ATLAS OF CHINA

Index Map

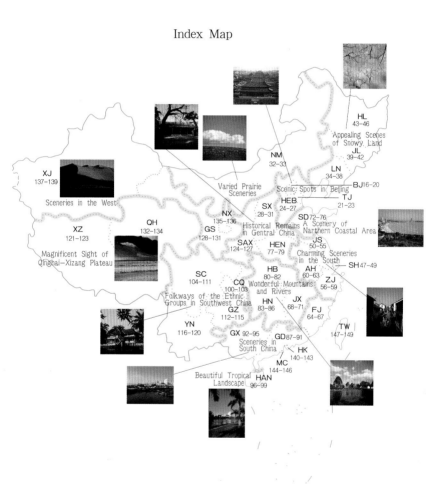

XJ
137–139

Sceneries in the West

XZ
121–123

Magnificent Sight of
Qinghai–Xizang Plateau

QH
132–134

NX
135–136

GS
128–131

SAX
124–127

Varied Prairie
Sceneries

NM
32–33

SX
28–31

Historical Remains
in Central China

HEN
77–79

HB
80–82

SC
104–111

CQ
100–103

Folkways of the Ethnic
Groups in Southwest China

GZ
112–115

YN
116–120

HN
83–86

GX 92–95

Sceneries in
South China

Wonderful Mountains
and Rivers

JX
68–71

GD 87–91

HK
140–143

MC
144–146

Beautiful Tropical
Landscape

HAN
96–99

HL
43–46

Appealing Scenes
of Snowy Land

JL
39–42

LN
34–38

Scenic Spots in Beijing

HEB
24–27

SD 72–76

A Scenery of
Northern Coastal Area

JS
50–55

Charming Sceneries
in the South

AH
60–63

ZJ
56–59

FJ
64–67

SH 47–49

TW
147–149

BJ 16–20

TJ
21–23

STAR MAP PRESS

图书在版编目（CIP）数据

中国旅行地图册:中英文/星球地图出版社编. - 北京:
星球地图出版社，2001.9
ISBN 7-80104-510-6

Ⅰ．中… Ⅱ．星… Ⅲ． 旅行图-中国-中英文
Ⅳ．K992.9

中国版本图书馆CIP数据核字（2000）第52052号

Tourist Atlas of China
(English Edition)
*

Compiled and Published by the Star Map Press
(69 Beisanhuan Zhonglu, Beijing. Postcode: 100088)
Printed by No.1206 Map Reproduction Plant, P.L.A.
Distributed by Xinhua Bookstore
*

First Edition, September 2001, Second Impression, January 2003
Format: 787 × 1092   1/24 7 Printing Sheets
Impression: 5001-10000
Price: 36.00 Yuan

CONTENTS

LEGEND

北京 Beijing ◎ — Capital / Foreign Capital

西安 Xi'an ◉ — Province-level Administrative centre

宝鸡 Baoji ◎ Xihai — Prefecture-level Administrative Centre

Lantian ◉ — County-level Administrative Centre

Zhaozhuang ○ — Township or Village

Under Construction — Railway

Under Construction — Expressway

102 — Main Road with Number, Flyover

Other Road and Pass

138 (205) Nautical Mile (km) — Shipping Route and Mileage

⚓ ⊤ ✈ — Port Wharf Airport

International Boundary, Undefined

Provincial Boundary

Boundary of Special Administrative Region

Boundary of Special Region

Cease-fire Line

Boundary of Nature Reserve

River Reservoir Waterfall

Salt Pan Lake

Canal Ditch

Well Spring

Great Wall

Nature Reserve included in "Man and Biosphere" of UN

Nature Reserves: National, Other

National Major Famous Scenic Area

National Tourist Resort

▲1998 — Peak with Elevation

Temple、Shrine

Pagoda

Grottoes

Ancient Tomb

Pavilion、Terrace or Tower

Monument

Great Wall、Pass

Cave、Limestone Cave Forest Park

Memorial Site Historic Site

Church、Mosque

Garden Scenic Spot

Expressway

National Road

Subway with Station

Transit Route for Other City's Vehicles

Business Street

Cableway

Ancient City Wall

Guesthouse, Hotel Library, Museum, Exhibition Hall

Bus Terminal Stadium

T.V. Station P.& T. Office

Hospital School

Bathing Beach Amusement Park

Scientific Research Institute Hi-tech Development Area

Beihai Park — Park and Urban Afforested Area

NATIONAL TOURISM ADMINISTRATION'S
TOURIST AGENCIES STATIONED ABROAD

NAME	ADDRESS	TELEPHONE
China Travel Agency in New York	350 Fifth Avenue,Suite 6413	001−212−7608218
	Empire State Building	001−212−7609700
	New York NY 10118 U.S.A.	001−212−7601710
China Travel Agency in Los Angeles	333 West Broadway,	001−818−5457507
	Suite 201 Glendale,	001−818−5457504
	CA91204 U.S.A.	001−818−5457505
China Travel Agency in London	4 Glentworth St, London	0044−171−9359787
	NW1 5PG	
China Travel Agency in Paris	15,Rue De Berri 75008	0033−1−56591010
	Paris France	
China Travel Agency in Sydney	Level 1944 Market Street	0061−2−92994057
	Sydney 2000 Australia	
China Travel Agency in Tokyo	Air China Bldg.8F,2−5−2	0081−3−5918686
	Toranomon Minato−Ku,	
	Tokyo Japan 105	
China Travel Agency in Frankfurt	Ilkenhans str 6	0049−69−520135
	D−60433 Frandkurt am Main	
	Deutschland	
China Travel Agency in Madrid	Gran VIa 88,Grupo 2,Planta	0034−1−5480011
	16 28010 Madrid Espana	
China Travel Agency in Singapore	1 Shenton Way,# 17−05	0065−2218681/82
	Robina House,Singapore 068803	
China Travel Agency in Osaka	OCAT 4F Ocat Building,	0081−6−6353280
	1−4−1 Minatomachi,	
	Naniwa−Ku,Osaka, Japan	
China Travel Agency in Zurich	Genfer Str 21 CH−8002 Zurich	0041−1−2018877
China Travel Agency in Toronto	480 University Ave,Suite 806	001−416−5996636
	Toronto,Ontario M5G 1V2,	
	Canada	
CITS Co. Ltd,HK.	Rm 1213−15&13 Floor,	00852−27325888 (Tel. exchange)
	Tower A,New Mandarin PIaza	
	14,Science Museum Road,	
	Tsimshatsui, Kowloon, Hong	
	Kong	

2

1:23300000

Scale 0   233   466   699 km

Survey Situated in the eastern part of Asia and the west coast of the Pacific Ocean,The People's Repubic of China,also being called China for short, is about 5500 km in length from the northernmost point in the main channel of the Heilong River north of Mohe City to the southernmost Zengmu Ansha Island , and 5200 km in width from Pamir Plateau in the west to the confluence of the Heilong River and Wusuli River in the east. China has a land area of about 9.6 million km², ranking the third in the world,and a large popu-lation of 1.2953 billion,of wich the Hans make-up more than 90%.

China has a land boundary of over 20000 km and neighbours D.P.R. Korea in the east,Russia and Mogolia in the north,Kazak-hstan and Kyrgyzstan in the northwest , Tajikistan, Afghanistan, Pakistan in the west , India , Nepal , Sikkim in the southwest, Myanmar, Laos ,Vietnam in the south,and faces Japan,R.O.Korea, Philippines, Indonesia, Malaysia across the seas .China has a con-tinental coastline of over 18000 km and is fringed by Bohai Sea, Huanghai Sea (Yellow Sea) , Donghai Sea (East Chira Sea) Nanhai Sea(South China Sea) from north to south and the territorial waters is 12 nautical miles in width.

3

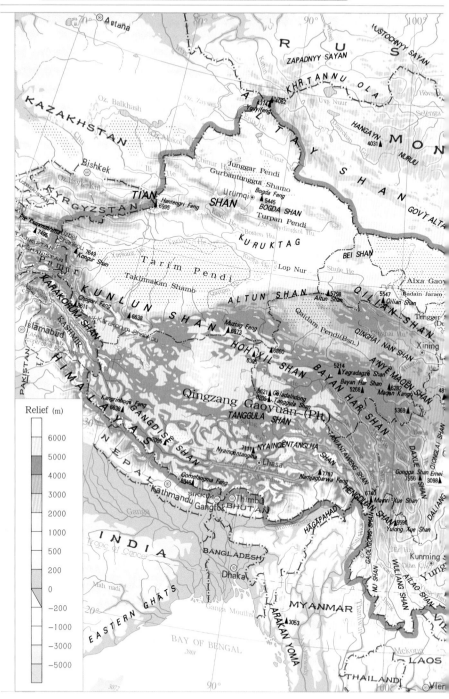

Natural Environment   China has a varied topography, with mountainous areas, plateaux and hilly areas occupying 2/3 of the total land. The terrain of China slopes from west to east, forming a flight of three steps. The first step consists of the Qinghai–Xizang(Tibet) Plateau , with an elevation of over 4000 metres above sea level, where stand Mts. Kunlun, Mts. Tanggula,   Mts. Gangdise, Mts.Nyainqentanglha, Mts.Karakorum.The second step includes the Yun–Gui Plateau, the Loess Plateau, Nei Mongol Plateau, Tarim Basin, Jungar Basin and Sichuan Basin. The third   step refers the vast area east of the Great Hinggan Ridge—Mt.Taihang—Mt.Wushan—Mt.   Xuefeng, mainly consisting of the Main Three Plains and the hilly land including the Nanling Ridge, Great Hinggan Ridge, Changbai Mountain and Mt. Taiwan. Along the coast, there exist about   6000 islands,among whichTaiwan Island is the largest.

1:23000000

Scale

0   230   460   690km

China possesses numerous rivers and most of famous rivers rise in the Qinghai–Xizang Plateau. The Changjiang(Yangtze) River,Huanghe River,together with the Lancang River, Zhujiang River, Huaihe River,Haihe River,Liaohe River and Heilongjiang River,belong to the Pacific river system, and the Nujiang River, Yarlung Zangbo River flow into the Indean Ocean, the Ertix River runs northward into the Arctic Ocean. The Grand Canal is the longest canal in the world, while the Tarim River is the longest continental river.

There exist more than 2800 lakes with a surface of over 1 km². Most of the freshwater lakes amass in the middle and lower reaches of the Changjiang(Yangtze) River. Numerous salt lakes lie on the Qinghai–Xizang Plateau, of which Qinghai Lake is the largest and Nam Co is a lake with the highest elevation in the world.

中国铁路 RAILWAYS OF CHINA

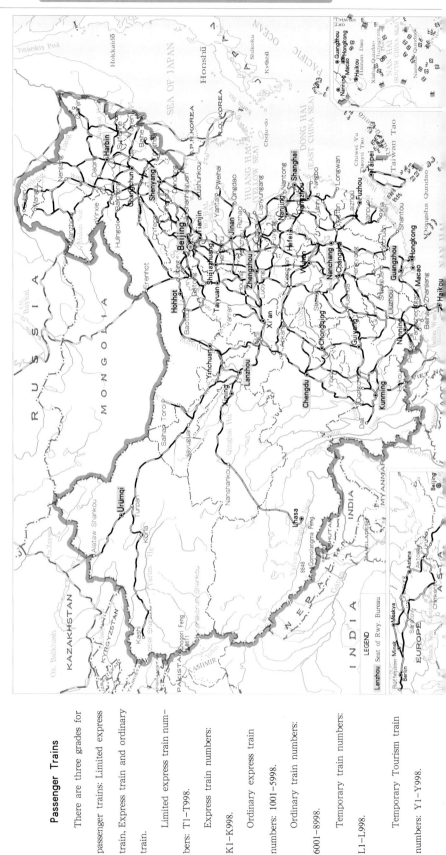

Passenger Trains

There are three grades for passenger trains: Limited express train, Express train and ordinary train.

Limited express train numbers: T1–T998.

Express train numbers: K1–K998.

Ordinary express train numbers: 1001–5998.

Ordinary train numbers: 6001–8998.

Temporary train numbers: L1–L998.

Temporary Tourism train numbers: Y1–Y998.

中国公路 HIGHWAYS OF CHINA

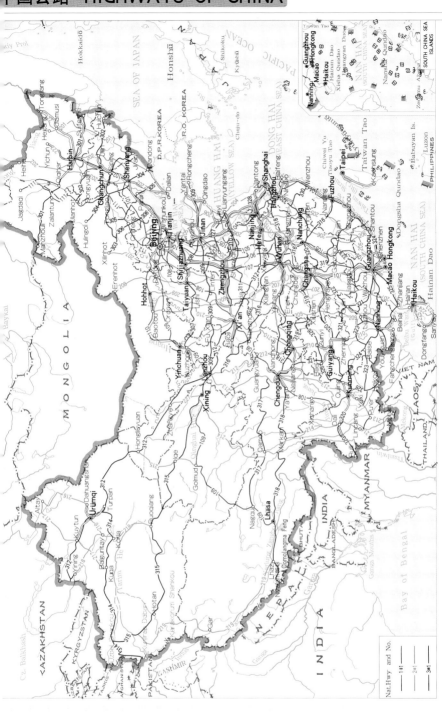

National Highway System of China

China's national highway system has been designed in a radiating and netted form, and the highways have been numbered in three different ways. The highways radiating from Beijing, the capital of China, are numbered clockwise from 101 to 112.The serial numbers of the highways running from north to south are 201 to 228, numbered from east to west, while the serial numbers of the highways running from east to west are 301 to 330, numbered from north to south.

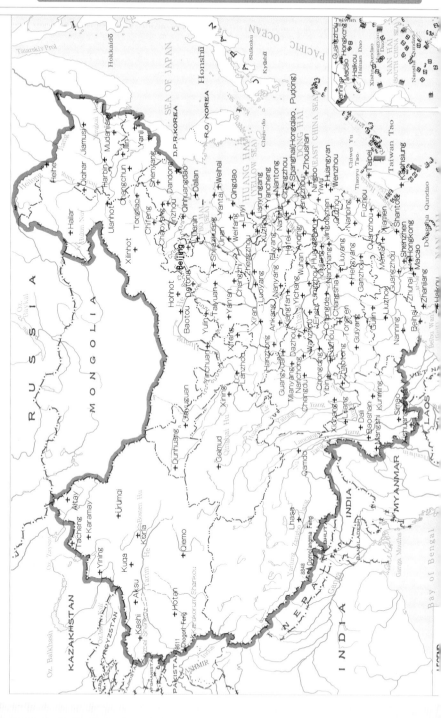

Airline codes:

CA : Air China

WH : China Northwest Airlines

CZ : China Southern Airlines

SZ : China Southwest Airlines

MU : China Eastern Airlines

CJ : China Northern Airlines

F6 : China National Aviation Corporation

XO : Xinjiang Airlines

3Q : Yunnan Airlines

MF : Xiamen Airlines Ltd.

3U : Sichuan Airlines

FM : Shanghai Airlines

G8 : Greatwall Airlines

WU : Wuhan Airlines

G4 : Guizhou Airlines

HU : Hainan Airlines

XW : China Xinhua Airlines

4G : Shenzhen Airlines

2Z : Chang'an Airlines

IV : Fujian Airlines

SC : Shangdong Airlines

8C : Shanxi Airlines

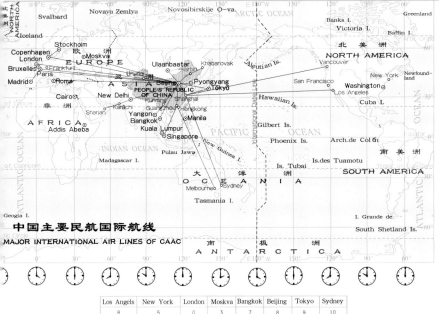

中国主要民航国际航线
MAJOR INTERNATIONAL AIR LINES OF CAAC

Los Angels	New York	London	Moskva	Bangkok	Beijing	Tokyo	Sydney
8	5	0	3	7	8	9	10
HOURS	SLOW				HOURS	FAST	

national Air Lines of China's Civil Aviation

g to: Amsterdam,Oakland,Bangkok,Brusselles,
openhangen, Frankfurt, Ha Noi, Fukuoka,
iroshima, Karachi, Kuala Lumpur, Kuwait,
ondon,Los Angeles,Madrid,Manila,Melbourne,
ilan, Moskva, Munich, Osaka, Paris, Pusan,
yongyang, Yangon, Rome, San francisco,
endai, Seoul, Singapore, Sydney, Tokyo,
laanbaatar, Vancouver, Stockholm.

hai to: Bangkok,Fukuoka,Hiroshima,Nagoya,
iigata,Okinawa, Osaka, Pusan, Sendai,Singapore,
okyo,Oakland,Brusseles,Frankfurt,Fukushima,
os Angeles,Madrid,Munich,Nagasaki,Sydney,
kayama,Paris,Phnom Penh,Vacouver.

gdu to: Bangkok,Singapore.

Chongqing to: Bangkok,Nagoya,Seoul.

Dalian to: Fukuoka, Hiroshima, Osaka, Pyongyang,
Sendai, Seoul,Tokyo, Toyama.

Guangzhou to: Amsterdam, Bangkok,Seoul, Singapore,
Kuala Lumpur,Melbourne,Osaka,Phnom Penh,
Ho Chi Minh City,Sydney,Jakarta.

Harbin to: Khabarovsk,Niigata,Vladivostok,Seoul.

Kunming to: Bangkok, Yangon, Seoul,Singapore,Vientiane

Qingdao to: Fukuoka,Pusan,Seoul.

Shenyang to: Irkutsk,Osaka,Pyongyang,Sapporo,Seoul,
Vladivostok.Irkutsk.

Tianjin to: Nagoya.

Ürümqi to: Almaty, Bishkek,Islamabad,Moskva,
Novosibirsk,Sharjah,Sverdlovsk,Tashkent.

Xi'an to: Seoul,Hiroshima,Nagoya,Niigata,Fukuoka.

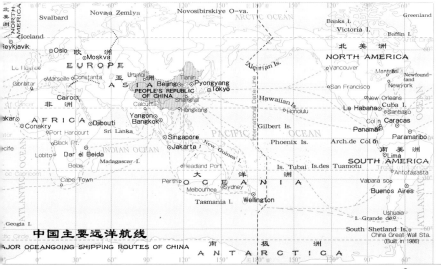

中国主要远洋航线
MAJOR OCEANGOING SHIPPING ROUTES OF CHINA

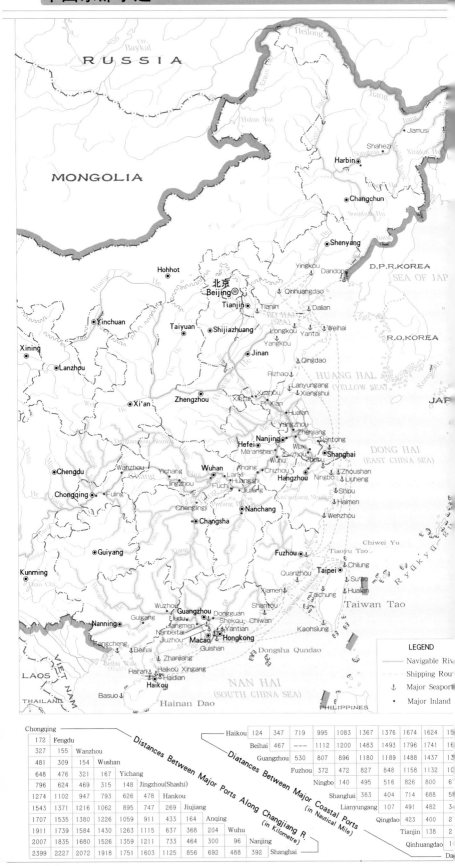

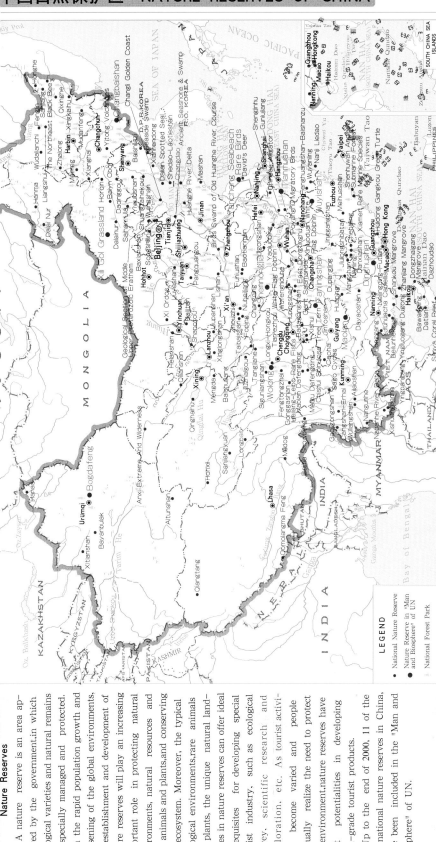

Nature Reserves

A nature reserve is an area approved by the government,in which biological varieties and natural remains are specially managed and protected. With the rapid population growth and worsening of the global environments, the establishment and development of nature reserves will play an increasing important role in protecting natural environments, natural resources and rare animals and plants,and conserving the ecosystem. Moreover, the typical ecological environments,rare animals and plants, the unique natural landscapes in nature reserves can offer ideal prerequisites for developing special tourist industry, such as ecological survey, scientific research and exploration, etc. As tourist activities become varied and people gradually realize the need to protect the environment,nature reserves have great potentialities in developing high-grade tourist products.

Up to the end of 2000, 11 of the 143 national nature reserves in China, have been included in the "Man and Biosphere" of UN.

11

LEGEND

Xi'an	Ancient Capital
Palace Museum	World Heritage
Xianyang	Famous Historic-Cultural City
Dianchi	National Tourist Resort

Three Major Palatial Architectural Complexes

Confucian Temple in Qufu

Daimiao Temple in Taishan Mountain

Imperial Palace in Beijing

Four Famous Towers

Huanghe (Yellow Crane) Tower in Wuhan

Tengwang Pavilion in Nanchang

Yueyang Tower in Hunan

Penglai Pavilion in Yantai

Four Famous Taoist Mountains

Wudang Mountain in Hubei Province

Longhu Mountain in Jiangxi Province

Qiyun Mountain in Anhui Province

Qingcheng Mountain in Sichuan Province

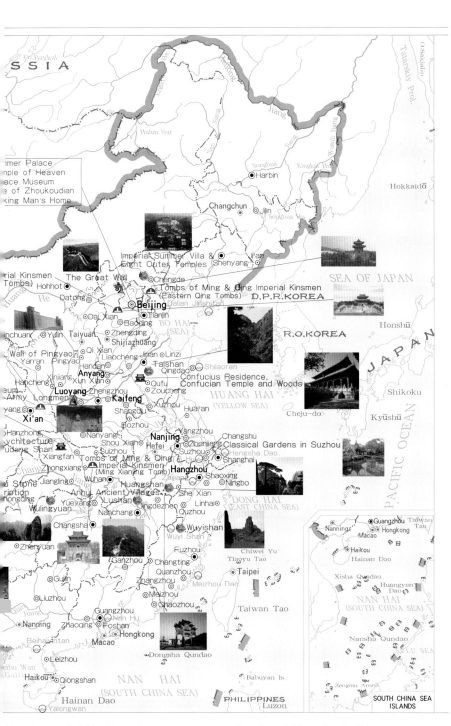

Four Famous Buddhist Mountains

Wutai Mountain in Shanxi Province

Jiuhua Mountain in Anhui Province

Putuo Mountain in Zhejiang Province

Emei Mountain in Sichuan Province

Four Famous Grottoes

Mogao Grottoes in Dunhuang

Longmen Grottoes in Luoyang

Yungang Grottoes in Datong

Maijishan Grottoes

Five Sacred Mountains in China

The Eastern Mountain-Taishan Mountain

The Sounthern Mountain-Hengshan Mountain

The Western Mountain-Huashan Mountain

The Northern Mountain-Hengshan Mountain

The Central Mountain-Songshan Mountain

21 Major Tourist Cities

Beijing

Chengde in Hebei Province

Harbin in Heilongjiang Province

Shanghai

Dalian in Liaoning Province

Hangzhou in Zhejiang Province

Nanjing and Suzhou in
Jiangsu Province

Xiamen in Fujian Province

Qingdao in Shandong Province

Wuhan in Hubei Province

Zhangjiajie in Hunan Province

Guangzhou and Shenzhen in
Guangdong Province

Guilin in Guangxi Zuang Aut.Reg.

Sanya in Hainan Province

Chongqing

Chengdu in Sichuan Provin

Kunming in Yunnan Provin

Xi'an in Shaanxi Province

Dunhuang in Gansu Provin

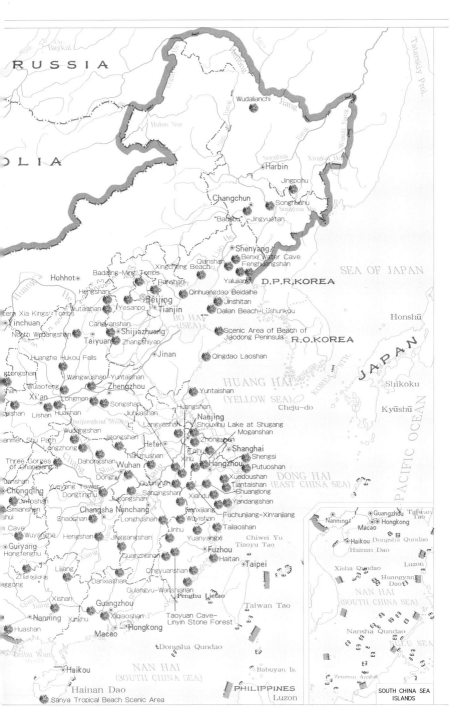

10 Major Scenic Areas

Wutai Mountain in Shanxi Province

Lushan Mountain in Jiangxi Province

Huashan Mountain in Shaanxi Province

Taishan Mountain in Shandong Province

Putuo Moutain in Zhejiang Province

Longmen Grottoes in Henan Province

Huangshan Mountain in Anhui Province

Emeishan Mountain in Sichuan Province

Wuyi Mountain in Fujian Province

Jiuzhaigou in Sichuan Province

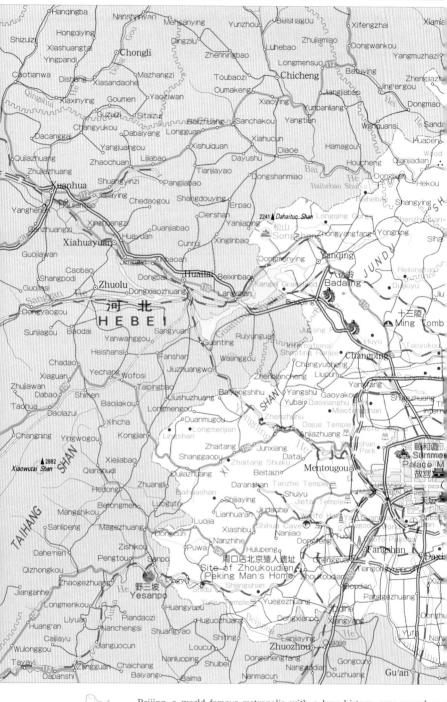

Beijing, a world famous metropolis with a long history, ever served as a dynastic capital from the beginning of the Jin in 1115 to the end of the Qin Dynasties in 1911. On October 1, 1949, the People's Republic of China was founded and Beijing has been the capital and the political, economic, communication, scientific and cultural centre of new China.

Beijing nestles at the foot of Yanshan Mountain on the northern tip of the North China Plain and mountainous areas make up 62% of its total land. It has a continental monsoon climate. The annual mean temperature is 11.8 ℃ and the annual

1:1050000

Scale 0   10.5   21.0   31.5 km

...pitation is 637 mm.

...Covering an area of 16800 km² and with a population of 12.46 million,
...g is one of the most important tourist cities of China. There are
...attractive historic sites and scenic spots, such as the Great Wall at
...ing, the Ming Tombs, Palace Museum, the site of Peking Man's Home
...houkoudian, the Summer Palace, Xiangshan Hill, Tian'anmen Square, the
...ple of Heaven, etc.

17

Summer Palace   Situated in northwest suburbs of Beijing, it use be an imperial garden and tempo palace in the Qing Dansty and consists Wanshou(Longevity) Hill and Kunn Lake.

Tian'anmen   Tian'anmen is the front gate of the Forbidd City. It has five openings and a magnificent gate tower, and is place where Chairman Mao Zedong proclaimed the founding of t People's Republic of China. From then on, Tian'anmen has beco the national symbol of China.

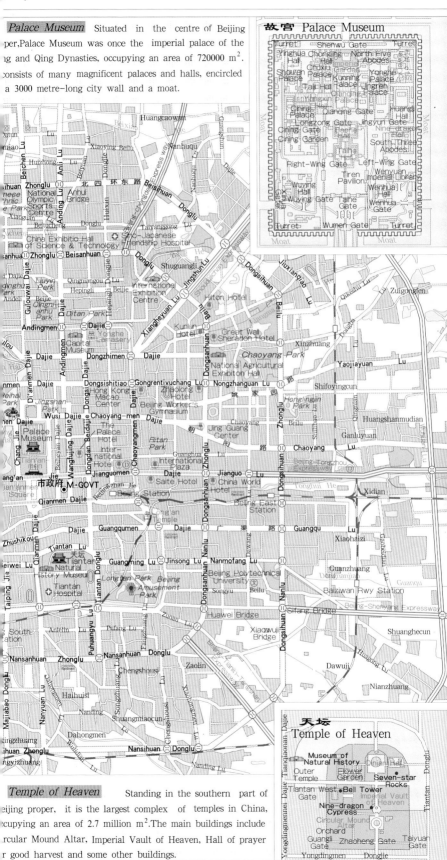

Palace Museum Situated in the centre of Beijing proper, Palace Museum was once the imperial palace of the Ming and Qing Dynasties, occupying an area of 720000 m^2. It consists of many magnificent palaces and halls, encircled by a 3000 metre-long city wall and a moat.

Temple of Heaven Standing in the southern part of Beijing proper, it is the largest complex of temples in China, occupying an area of 2.7 million m^2. The main buildings include Circular Mound Altar, Imperial Vault of Heaven, Hall of prayer for good harvest and some other buildings.

Ming Tombs Situated at the foot of Tiansh Mountain in Changping County, it is the burial site of Ming emperors and 23 empresses, and the best-preserv imperial tombs, covering an area of 40 km². Among thirteen tombs, Changling Tomb is the largest and me magnificent. The Ling'en Hall of Changling Tomb is t biggest wooden structure in China. Dingling Tomb lies the southwest of Changling Tomb, of which the highlig is its underground palace. More than 3000 pieces of precid historical relics were unearthed. In 1959, a museum w established at the site of Dingling Tomb, since then, Mi Tombs have become one of the most famous tourist are

The Great Wall at Badaling First built over 2C years ago, the Great Wall is reputed as a wonder of t world. Lying in Yanqing County northwest of Beijir Badaling section of the Great Wall is quite magnifice and typical among the Ming Great Walls. This section the Great Wall was built with giant stone slabs a specially-made bricks, with watch towers, embrasures a drainage system. The Wall is 6-7 metres high and more than 5 metres wide at the top, with beacd towers built at nearby places with broad view for sending signals during wartime. Now, a Great Wa Museum, a cable way and some other buildings have been set up in this area.

天津市 TIANJIN MUNICIPALITY

Scale 1:1350000

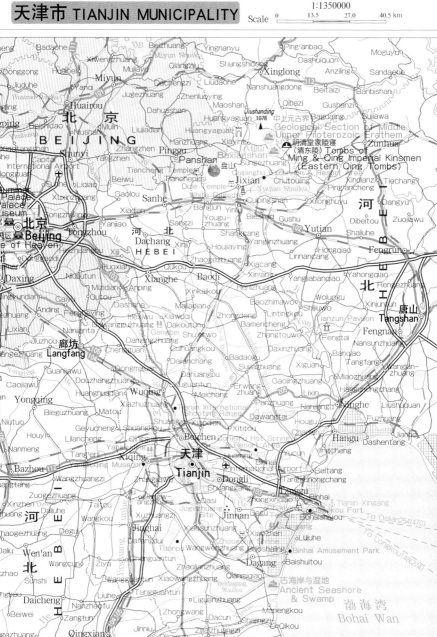

Situated in the lower reaches of the Haihe River and facing the Bohai Sea to the east , Tianjin is the important industrial and commercial centre in North China , one of the four municipalities directly under the central government. Area : over 11000 km².

Tianjin has a relative flat terrain sloping from north to south. It enjoys distinct four seasons in a year,but autumn is the best season. The annual mean temperature is about 13℃ , and the annual precipitation is 500~700 mm.

Tianjin is a famous cultural city with a long history . The main scenic sites   include Mt.Panshan Scenic Area , Dule Temple , Huangyaguan Great Wall , Wanghai Tower and Dagukou Fort. Besides, Confucian Temple, Grand Mosque, Food Street and Ancient Cultural Street are also interesting places.

The specialities in Tianjin include Tianjin carpet, Yangliuqing New Year Pictures, ect.

天津
TIANJIN

Tianjin Institute of Commerce

Institute of Agricultural Science

Memorial Hall of Ping-Jin Campaign

Zhaozhuangzi

Dabianzhuang   Brewery

Lijiayuan

Xijiangjing

Chuanfuxincun

Tianhuan Bus Terminal

Jinjinggongle Flyover   Fukanglu Flyover

Huayuan Industry Area

Huayuan Residential Area

Hebei Polytechnical University

Dingzigu Post Office

Xigu Park

Dongyuzhuang

Xizhan Bus Terminal

Tianjin West Station

West Station

Hongqiao Stadium

Grand Mosque

Minzugong

Tianjin North Static

Dabei Temple

Santiaoshi History Museum

Wanghailou Cathedral

Shizilin Daji

Jieyuan Dao   北马路 Bei Malu

Yihetuan Memorial Hall

Fenshui Dao

Yanhualou Restaurant

Huanghe   Dao

Changhong Park

Tianjin Hotel

Confucian Temple

Opera Museum

Nan   Malu

Nanmen Hotel

Dongbeijiao Bus Terminal

Ancient Cultural Street

Central Square

Changjiang Dao   Sanmalu

Nankai People's Cultural Palace

Xihu   Dao

Jialefu Nankai Store   Institute of T.C.M.

Anshan   Xidao

Tianjin University

Nankai University

No.1 Central Hospital

Baoshan Dao

Chuxiong Dao

Fu'an   Dao

XKai Cathedral   Yingkou

Nanjing Lu

Renmin Stadium

Tianyu Hotel

Medical University

Tianhai Hotel

Fukang Lu   Wujiayao Dajie

Tianjin Library

South Bailai Bus Terminal

Children's Amusement Park

Museum of Natural History

Yangliuqing Industrial Exhibition Hall

Shredon Hote

Tianjin Ho

Wangdingdi Hotel

Hubinyuan Restaurant

Zhou Enlai, Deng Yingchao Memorial Hall

水上公园
Shuishang Park

Zoo

Lida Bar

Binshui

International Exhibition Ce

Institute of Physical Culture

Liqizhuang Post Office

盘山
Mt. Panshan   Guayue Peak

Yunzhao Temple   Suspending Rock

Wansong Temple   Pangu Temple   Taoyuan Cave   Shangfang Temple

Dobaota Pagoda

Dongganjian   Toad-like Rock

Bayin Cave   Snake-like Rock

Tiancheng Temple   Xiganjian   Shaolin Temple

Guest-Greeting Pine

Martyrs' Cemetery

Mt.Panshan Situated ab
125 km from Tianjin, Mt.Pansha
is one of the famous mountains
China and a national scenic ar
and is reputed as the Fi
Mountian east of Beijing . It h
five peaks,including Guayue Pea
Zigai Peak , Zilai Peak , Jiuhua
Peak and Wujian Peak.

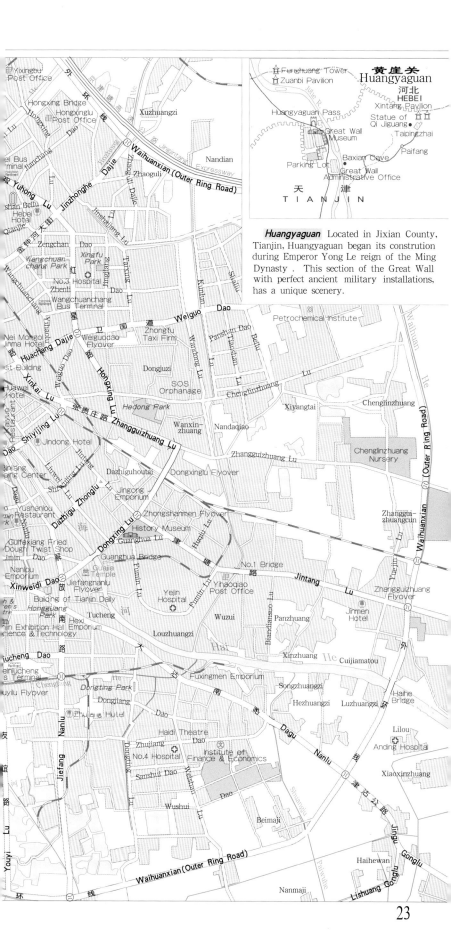

23

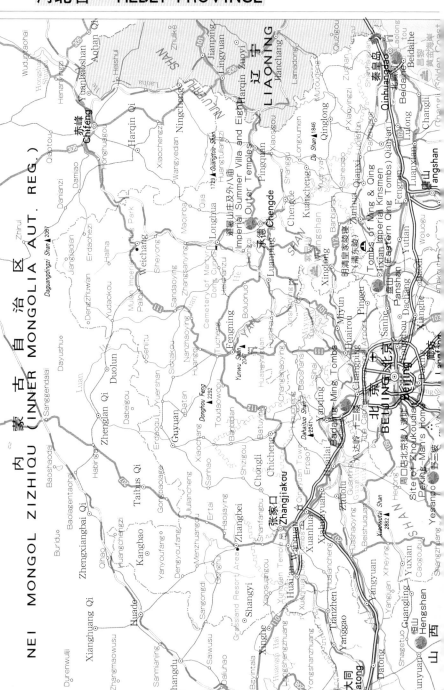

Situated in the northern part of North China Plain on the Bohai Se, Hebei Province is bounded by the Provinces of Liaoning, Shanxi, Hena, Shandong and Nei Mongol Autonomous Region. Area: 190000 km².

Hebei consists of two sections: Hebei Plain (a part of North China Plai, in the east and south, and the mountain ranges along the northern and west frontiers.

It has a semi-humid and semi-arid continental climate, with an une distribution of rainfall. The annual mean temperature is 0-14°C and the annual precipitation is 3, 800 mm.

Hebei Province possesses rich tourist resources. The Imperial Summer Villa and Eight Outer Te

s in Chengde, the summer resort of Qinhuangdao–Beidaihe, Mt. Cangyan,
...angshi Crag and Yesanpo are all national major famous scenic areas,
...ong which, the Imperial Summer Villa and Eight Outer Temples have been
...d in the World Heritages. Besides, Mt. Taihang, Mt. Langya, Mt. Wuling,
... Eastern and Western Qing Tombs, etc, are also famous scenic spots and
...oric sites.

... Pear in Zhaozhou, peach in Shenzhou, grape in Xuanhua, etc, are all famous
...l products. The handicraft articles, such as stone carving in Quyang, snuff bottle in Hengshui,
...d carving in Chengde, etc, are all well–known in China. Especially porcelain in Tangshan enjoys
...d fame, and Tangshan is known as one of the porcelain manufacture centre of China.

25

石家庄
SHIJIAZHUANG

清东陵
Eastern Qing Tombs

east of Beijing, it is the burial place for the members of the imperial family of the Qing Dynasty. This is a magnificent and complete imperial mausoleum, where there are five emperor tombs, four empress tombs and five imperial concumbine tombs. It is now one of the famous historic sites in China.

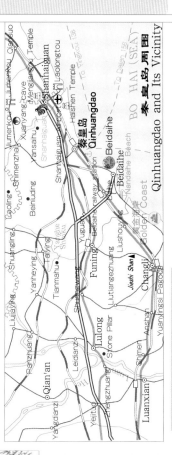

清西陵 Western Qing Tombs

Western Qing Tombs Lying at the foot of Mt .Yongning 15 km east of Yixian County and 120 km southwest of Beijing, it is the burial site for the members of the imperial family of the Qing Dynasty,where buried are four emperors. The tomb area is over 100 km in circumference. It is now a famous excursion site south of Beijing.

秦皇岛周围 Qinhuangdao and Its Vicinity

Qinhuangdao and Its Vicinity Qinhuangdao is a seaport city consisting of Shanhaiguan, Beidaihe, seaport district and Changli County. Shanhaiguan is a famous pass located at a strategic spot of the Great Wall between mountains and sea.It is renowned for its magnificent gatetower named No.1 Pass under Heaven. The well-known scenic spot Laolongtou is the starting point of the Great Wall.

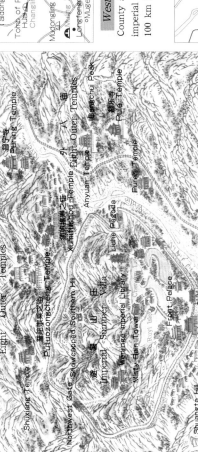

外 八 庙 Eight Outer Temples
避 暑 山 庄 Imperial Summer Villa
承德避暑山庄 Imperial Summer Villa in Chengde

Imperial Summer Villa in Chengde Imperial Summer Villa and Eight Outer Temples in Chengde are among the first group of the major scenic areas named by the State Council and form one of the ten famous scenic areas in China. In 1992, this scenic area was included in the List of World Heritages by UNESCO.

The Imperial Summer Villa, also called Rehe Temporary Palace, is located in Chengde City and is the largest imperial garden well preserved, occupying an area of 5.64 million m².

The Eight Outer Temples form the largest temple group built in the early period of the Qing Dynasty. The temples built in the Tibetan, Han and Mongolian styles are scattered among the nearby hills around the Summer Villa. In fact, there were orginally 11 temples, of which only seven remain now. The wooden statue of the Goddess of Mercy in Puning Temple is 22.2 metres high, the highest of its kind in China.

山西省　SHANXI PROVINCE

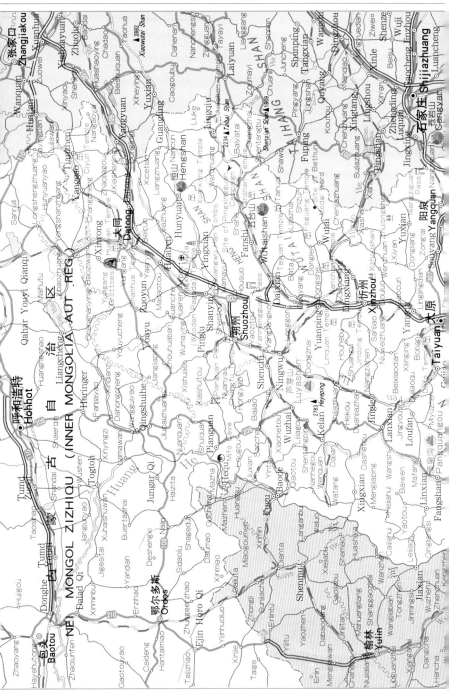

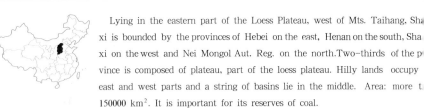

Lying in the eastern part of the Loess Plateau, west of Mts. Taihang, Sha
xi is bounded by the provinces of Hebei on the east, Henan on the south, Sha
xi on the west and Nei Mongol Aut. Reg. on the north. Two-thirds of the p
vince is composed of plateau, part of the loess plateau. Hilly lands occupy
east and west parts and a string of basins lie in the middle. Area: more t
150000 km². It is important for its reserves of coal.

    Shanxi has a temperate continental climate and four distinct seasons with
annual mean temperature of 4–14°C, and the annual precipitation is 400–600 mm.

    Shanxi is one of the birthplaces of the ancient civilization of the Chinese Nation. The natio

1:2800000

Scale 0 28 56 84 km

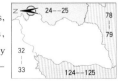

or famous scenic areas include Mt. Wutai, Mt. Hengshan, Hukou Falls, ...ngang Grottoes, etc. Shanxi is famous for its great number of temples, ...odas and frescoes, such as Jinci Temple, Wooden Pagoda in Yingxian County ... Guandi Temple in Xiezhou, etc. It is thus reputed as a "Museum of An-...t Arts".

The famous local products are Fenjiu Wine in Fenyang, the mature vinegar in Qingxu ...unty and date in Jishan, etc.

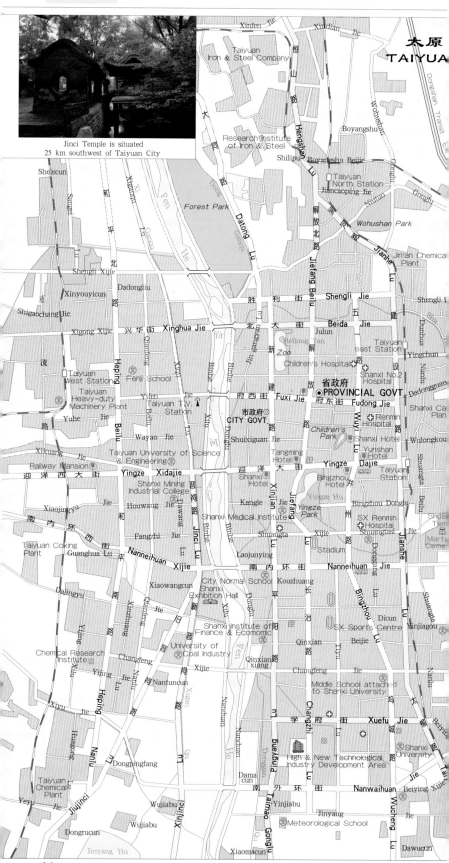

Jinci Temple is situated
25 km southwest of Taiyuan City

太原
TAIYUA

Xinfen Jie
Xindian Jie

Taiyuan
Iron & Steel Company

恒山路
Hengshan Lu

Dongsian Transit Ex

Boyangshu

Research Institute
of Iron & Steel

Shilipu Boyangshu Beijie

Taiyuan
North Station

Jiancaoping Jie

Niutuo

Gonghu

Wohushan Park

Shelecun

Sangci

Xi平路

Fen Jie

Dong Jie

Gantu Jie

Forest Park

Datong Lu

Jiefang Beilu

Jianhe Lu

Jin'an Chemica
Plant

Shengli Xijie

Xinyouyicun

Dadongliu

胜利街

Shengli Jie

Shengli I

Shigaochang Jie

Xigong Xijie

兴华街

Xinghua Jie

北大街

Beida Jie

建

Julun

Taiyuan
East Station

Yingchun

流

新建路

Heilong Tan
Zoo

解

放

Taiyuan
West Station

Fenji School

Yifen
Taiyuan T.V.
Station

Children's Hospital

省政府
PROVINCIAL GOVT

Shanxi No.2
Hospital

Dadongguan

Taiyuan
Heavy-duty
Machinery Plant

Yuhe Jie

府西街 Fuxi Jie

市政府
CITY GOVT

府东街 Fudong Jie

Shanxi Ca
Plan

Xikuang

Wayao Jie

Shuixiguan Jie

Renmin
Hospital

Shanxi Hotel

Wulongkou

Railway Mansion

Taiyuan University of Science
& Engineering

Children's
Park

Yunshan
Hotel

Yingze Xidajie

Yingze Xidajie

Shanxi Mining
Industrial College

Houwang Jie

Shanxi
Hotel

迎泽大街

Tangming
Hotel

Yingze

Bingzhou
Hotel

Dajie

Taiyuan
Station

Xiaojingyu

Jie

Fangzhi Jie

Jinci Lu

Shanxi Medical Institute

Shuangta

Yingze
Park

Bingzhou Donglu

SX Renmin
Hospital

Shual
Tem

Taiyuan Coking
Plant

Guanghua Lu

Nanneihuan Xijie

Laojunying

Xijie

Stadium

Nanneihuan Jie

Marty
Ceme

Dajingyu

Xiaowangcun

City Normal School Kouzhuang

Shanxi
Exhibition Hall

南内环街

SX Sports Centre

Dicun

Xinjiagou

Chemical Research
Institute

Changfeng

Shanxi Institute of
Finance & Economic

University of
Coal Industry

Qinxian

Qinxian
xiang

Beijie

Xiru Jie

Nantuncun

Xijie

Changfeng Jie

Middle School attached
to Shanxi University

Dongpingfang

学府街

Xuefu Jie

Taiyuan
Chemical
Plant

Jiujinci

Wujiabu

High & New Technological
Industry Development Area

Shanxi
University

Yeyu Jie

Dongrucun

Wujiabu

Dama
cun

南外环街

Nanwaihuan

Beiying Xijie

Yinjiabu

Jinyang

Meteorological School

Dawucun

Jinyang Hu

Xiaomacun

五台山
Mt. Wutai

Mt. Wutai Situated in the northeast of Wutai County , Mt.Wutai is one of the four famous ountains to the Buddhists and has five terrace-like peaks, inclding Wanghai Peak in the east, Guayue ak in the west, Jinxiu Peak in the south, Yedou Peak in the north and Cuiyan Peak standing in the ntral part. From May to August every year, it is the best period for tourism.

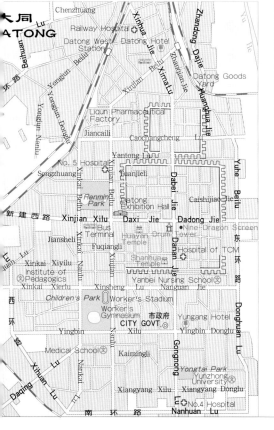

Yungang Grottoes Located at the southern foot of Mt. Wuzhou, 16 km west of Datong City,Yungang grottoes, one of China's four cave groups with Buddhist statues,were first hewn in the Northern Wei Dynasty. Now, there are still more than fifty grottoes housing 51000 Buddha statues. The distinguished art style of the statues shows the integration of the Qin and Han traditions with the foreign cultural essences . After the founding of the People's Republic of China, a special preservation office was set up, and the Grottoes are now under the State protection.

31

Hohhot

呼和浩特
Hohhot

Lying in the northern border area of China, it is the first autonome region in the country, which was set up on May 1, 1947, and is inhabited about 80 percent of the population of the Mongolian nationality in China. T Region borders on Gansu, Ningxia, Shaanxi, Shanxi, Hebei, Liaoning, Jilin, and Mongolia and Russia. Area: more than 1180000 km^2.

Nei Mongol is essentially an inland plateau with a flat surface and fring by mountains and valleys.

It enjoys a continental monsoon climate of the temperate zone, with a long and cold win but a pleasant summer. The annual mean temperature is $-1-10^\circ C$, and the annual precipitatior.

1:9250000
Scale 0   92.5   185.0   277.5 km

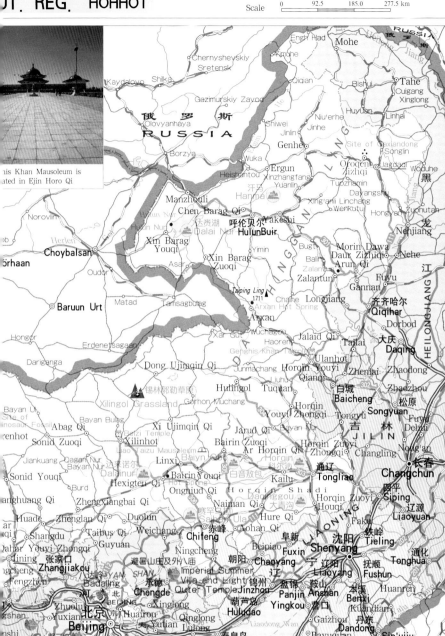

...his Khan Mausoleum is ...ated in Ejin Horo Qi

...450 mm.

Because of its vast area belonging to the plateau grassland landscape, ...efore, the tourist resources consist mainly of beautiful grassland scenery and ... Mongolian ethnic culture. Summer and autumn are the best seasons for ...ism.

The Region has a long history. Countless historic cultural relics and archaeogical studies have ...ved that it is one of the birthplaces of the Chinese nation. The Nadam Fair held in a period ...ween July and August every year is a good chance to enjoy the fascinating grassland scenery ...the local customs of the Mongolian nationality.

Shenyang Imperial Palace is situated in the centre of the old city proper

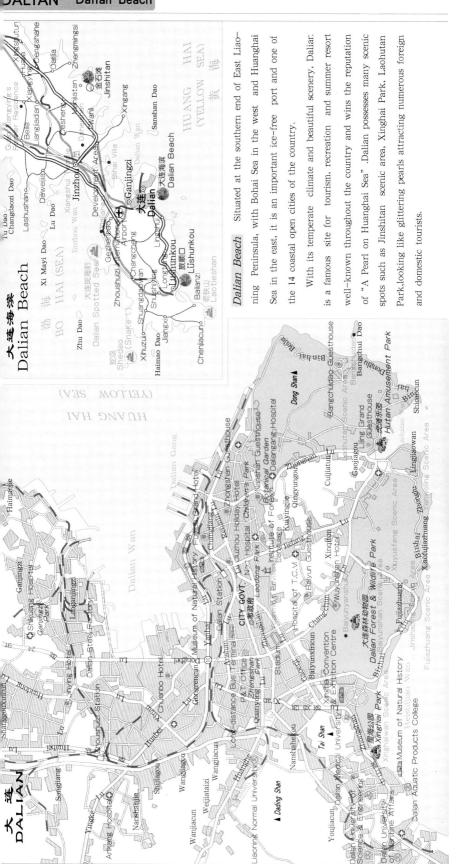

大连海滨
Dalian Beach

Dalian Beach　Situated at the southern end of East Liao-ning Peninsula, with Bohai Sea in the west and Huanghai Sea in the east, it is an important ice-free port and one of the 14 coastal open cities of the country.

With its temperate climate and beautiful scenery, Dalian is a famous site for tourism, recreation and summer resort well-known throughout the country and wins the reputation of "A Pearl on Huanghai Sea".Dalian possesses many scenic spots such as Jinshitan scenic area, Xinghai Park, Laohutan Park,looking like glittering pearls attracting numerous foreign and domestic tourists.

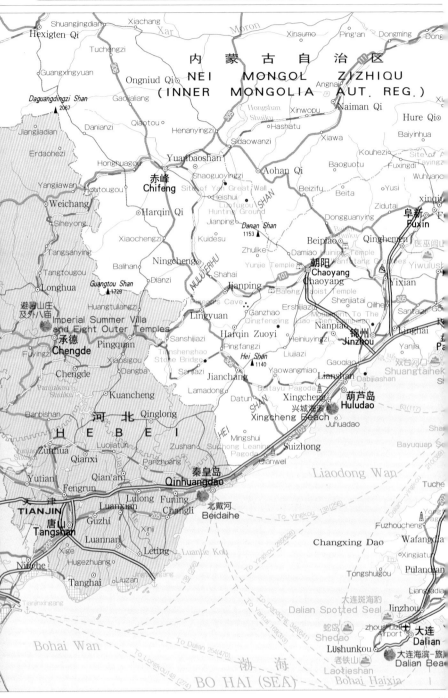

Situated in the southern part of Northeast China, Liaoning Province adj
D. P. R. Korea in the east, Hebei in the southwest, Nei Mongol Autonom
Region in the northwest and Jilin in the northeast. Area: about 150000 km

Liaoning consists essentially of a central lowland, flanked by mountains
highlands in the east and west respectively. A southward extension of the e
tern highlands form the Liaoning Peninsula.

The province enjoys a temperate continental climate, with a warm and ra
summer and a short but pleasant autumn. The annual mean temperature is 6-11°C and the ye
precipitation is 440-1130 mm.

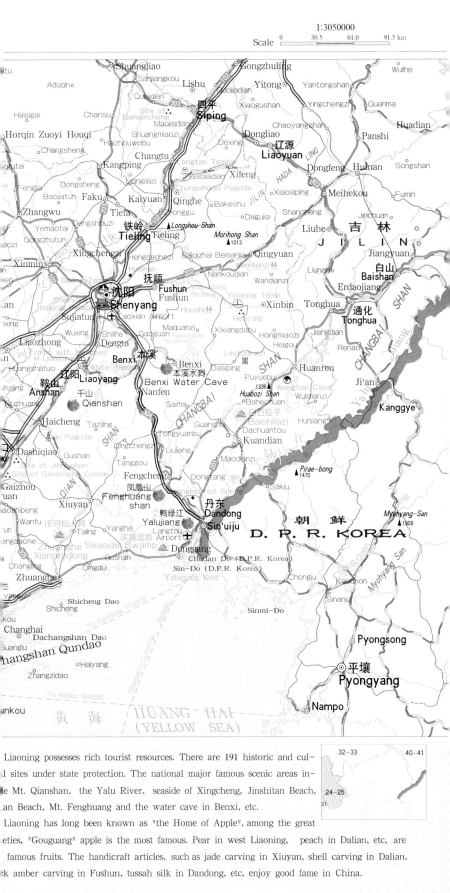

1:3050000

Scale 0   30.5   61.0   91.5 km

Liaoning possesses rich tourist resources. There are 191 historic and cul-
l sites under state protection. The national major famous scenic areas in-
e Mt. Qianshan, the Yalu River, seaside of Xingcheng, Jinshitan Beach,
an Beach, Mt. Fenghuang and the water cave in Benxi, etc.
Liaoning has long been known as "the Home of Apple", among the great
eties, "Gouguang" apple is the most famous. Pear in west Liaoning,   peach in Dalian, etc, are
famous fruits. The handicraft articles, such as jade carving in Xiuyan, shell carving in Dalian,
k amber carving in Fushun, tussah silk in Dandong, etc, enjoy good fame in China.

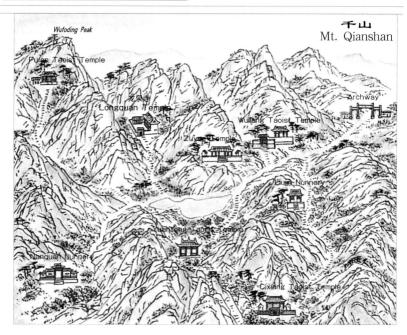

Mt. Qianshan　Situated 25 kilometers south of Anshan City, Mt. Qianshan is one of the three famous mountains and a famous scenic area in Northeast China.

In Mt.Qianshan Scenic Area, there are more than 180 scenic spots consisting mainly of exotic pine trees, rocks of grotesque shapes and ancient temples. The main scenic spots include 5 ancient temples, (Longquan, Xiangyan, Zhonghui, Da'an and Zhu-yue Temples) and 8 Taoist Temples, 9 palaces, 12 Buddhist convents, etc. Longquan Temple is the largest Buddhist temple in Mt. Qianshan built in the Tang Dynasty. Wuliang Taoist Temple standing in Beigou Valley is the largest Taoist religious edifice in that area, and it was the first built in the early Qing Dynasty.

Mt. Fenghuang　Located 2.5 kilometers southeast of Fenghuang Man Autonomous County, Liaoning Province, Mt. Fenghuang has a long history and a great number of historic sites and has long been known as the first famous mountain of the Great Wall and one of the four famous mountains in the province.It is famous for its high peaks, ancient temples and pagodas,stone inscriptions,clear springs and rare plants. The main scenic spots include Zanyun Peak, Qianyan Peak, Diecui Peak, etc.

Tianchi Lake on Mt.Changbai Lying in Mt.Changbai Nature Reserve, Tianchi Lake, a typical alpine lake, is the Sino-Korean border lake formed by volcanic eruption and the deepest crater lake with an elevation of 2155 m, covering an area of 9.2km². Around the lake, there stand 16 magnificent high peaks.

Tianchi Lake is enveloped by cloud and mist nearly all the year round and shows its true feature in a few days in summer,when the waters of the lake is as smooth as a mirror, reflecting the rocks and high cliffs around it.At the north bank of the lake, there is a gap from where the lake waters rush down the cliff, forming a 68 metres long waterfall.To the north of the lake, there are also other famous scenic spots, such as Bagui Temple, Niulangdu and Jinqian Spring, etc.

Songhua Lake Located in the upper reaches of the Songhua River, 24 km southeast of Jilin City,Songhua Lake is a man-made one where the famous Fengman Hydropower Station lies. The water surface of the lake totals 500 km² and the mirror-like water is encircled by peaks with grotesque shapes. In the lake, there are many islets,of which Wuhu (Five Tigers) Islet is the biggest. Viewing from the air, the islet looks like five tigers playing in the clear waters. Around the lake, forest occupies an area of about 550 km². Near the lake lies a large skiing ground, one of the largest in China.

Songhua Lake integrates the beautiful sceneries of Mt. Huangshan and the Lijiang River, and is a nice tourist site all the year round.

39

吉林省 JILIN PROVINCE

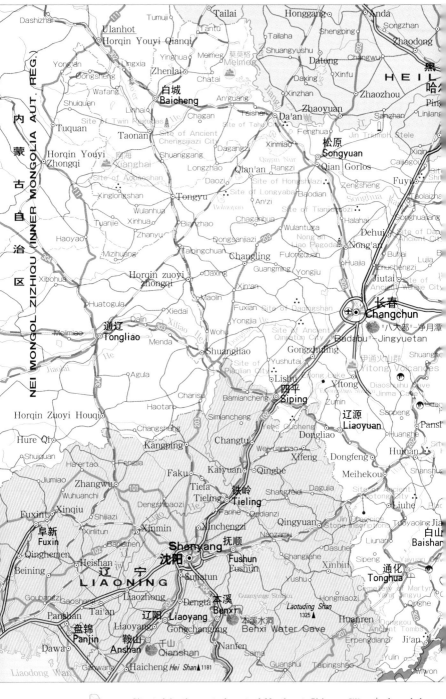

Situated in the central part of Northeast China, Jilin is bounded on
south by Liaoning, on the north by Heilongjiang, on the west by Nei Mon
and by the Russian Federation on the east, and faces Democratic Peop
Republic of Korea across the Yalu River. Area:more than 180000 km².

The province may be roughly divided into two parts:the eastern mountai
and the western plains. Mountainous and hilly areas occupy more than 60%
its land.

Jilin has a long and cold winter but a pleasant summer. The annual mean temperature is −3
7°C. The beautiful snow scenery along the Songhua River and the Korean ethnic culture attra

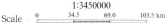

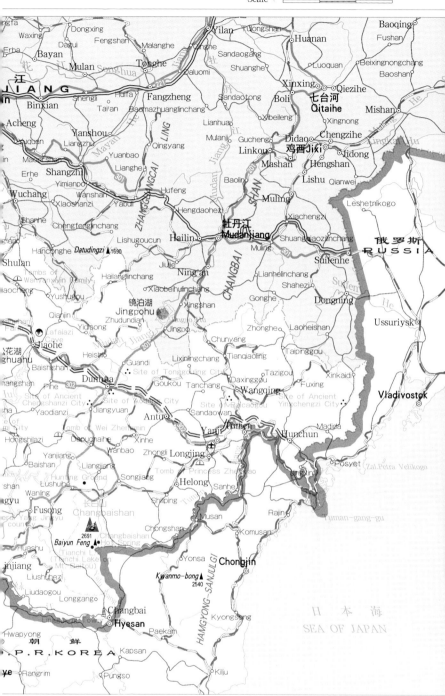

herous tourists.

Most of the tourist sites exist in the areas of Changchun city, Jilin city along the Songhua River–Mt. Changbai. Other scenic areas are distrib-in Yanbian, Tonghua,Ji'an,Siping, Baicheng and Liaoyuan. The major ous scenic areas are Songhua Lake, Badabu–Jingyuetan reservoir. Besides, Tianchi Lake on Mt. Changbai and the deer farm at the foot of Mt.longtan by the east bank he Songhua River, are also famous scenic areas.

There are many special local products in Jilin, in which, ginseng, pilose antler and marten fur the most famous.

哈尔滨
HARBIN

Harbin Ice & Snow Tourist Festival
is held from Jan.to Feb. every year

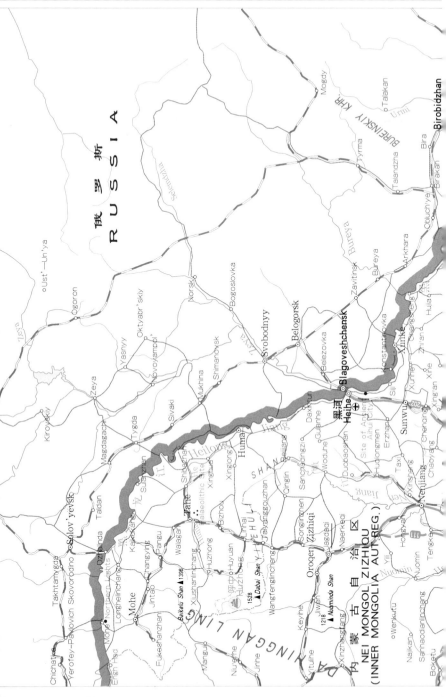

Situated in the northernmost part of China, Heilongjiang borders on Ji[...] Nei Mongol Autonomous Region and faces the Russian Federation across t[...] Heilong River and the Wusuli River. Area: about 450000 km^2.

The province has a terrain sloping slightly from northwest to southea[...] and the hilly lands and plains are distributed alternately. It has a long a[...] cold winter and a very short summer, with the annual mean temperature [...] -2 — $-3°C$.

Heilongjiang is one of the provinces in which more volcanoes remain. Volcanism has crea[...] many tourist sites, such as the Wudalianchi Lake. (five interlinked lakes) and the Jingpo La[...]

1:5650000

Scale 0   56.5   113.0   169.5 km

ic areas, etc. Because of its high latitudes and low temperature in winter,
ongjiang is the best place for viewing ice and snow scenery. The well-
wn Ice Lantern Show held in Harbin every year attracts a great number
ourists. Other interesting places are the underground lava caves and
erground forest near Jingpo Lake, Zhalong Nature Reserve near Qiqihar
, etc.

The province is one of the important bases of grain production and ginseng, pilose antler, sa-
etc, are the famous special local products.

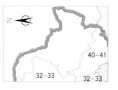

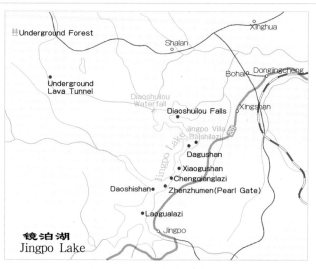

镜泊湖
Jingpo Lake

Jingpo Lake Situa
in the upper reaches of
Mudan River, Southwest
Ning'an County and ab
110 km away from Mudanjia
City, Jingpo Lake is the la
gest lava barrier lake
mountainous area in Chi
It is about 45 km long and 6
wide in maximum, and occu
ies a water surface of 90 k
Its unadorned beautiful sc
ery attracts more and m
tourists.

There exist eight famo
scenic spots in the lake are
including Diaoshuilou Fa
looking like a silver curtain, exquisite Zhenzhumen (pearl Gate), the lush Xiaogushan and Baishila
with numerous dwelling birds. There are also several volcanic scenic sites. The underground fore
(Crater forest) 45km away from Jingpo Lake, is the most famous.

Yabuli Skiing Ground   The skiing ground is
situated 194 km, southeast of Harbin, the capital of
Heilongjiang Province, with 15 skiing courses totaling
more than 30 km, where 95' Winter Asian Games was
held. It is the largest one in China, with the best
natural conditions and perfect faclities. Now, the skiing
ground is the best site for skiing-lovers during winter
time.

亚布力滑雪:
Yabuli Skiing Gro

Legend	High Grade Course	Cross-country Course
	Athletic Course	Cableway

Wudalianchi   Lying in the northern suburbs of Wudalianchi City,it is one of
the national major nature reserves and major famous scenic areas. Because of the volcanic eruptions in 1719-1721, the lava-flow covered an area of more than 60 km^2 and
the course of the Baihe River was dammed, forming five interlinked barrier Lakes.

五大连池
Wudalianchi

上海市 SHANGHAI MUNICIPALITY

Scale 1:1150000

0 11.5 23.0 km

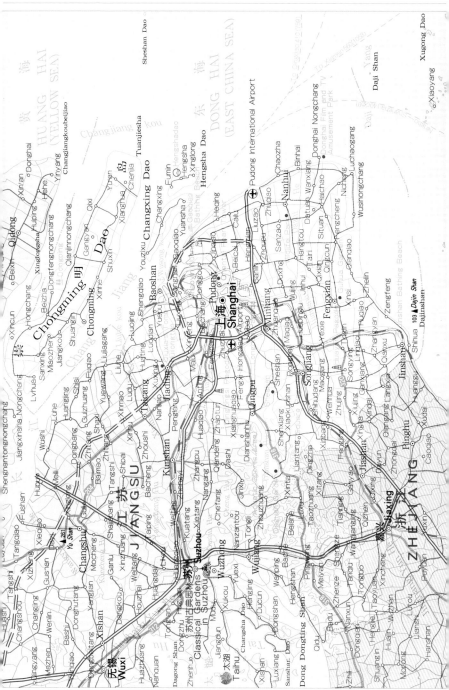

Located at the confluence of the Changjiang River and Qiantang River, Shanghai is one of the four municipalties directly under the Central Government and China's largest city. Area: over 6000 km². Shanghai occupies a part of the alluvial plain of the Changjiang Delta, It has a temperate and humid climate, with an annual mean temperature of 15.7 ℃ and an annual precipitation of 1100 mm.

Shanghai is the hub of the land and waterway communications,civil aviaton of East China,and major centre of industry, commerce, foreign trade,science and technology of China. It is also the thplace of the Chinese Communist Party.The famous scenic spots include Yuyuan Market, Yufo mple,the site of the First National Conference of CPC and the former residence of Sun Yat-sen.

47

SHANGHAI

Nanjing Lu

Yuyuan Market

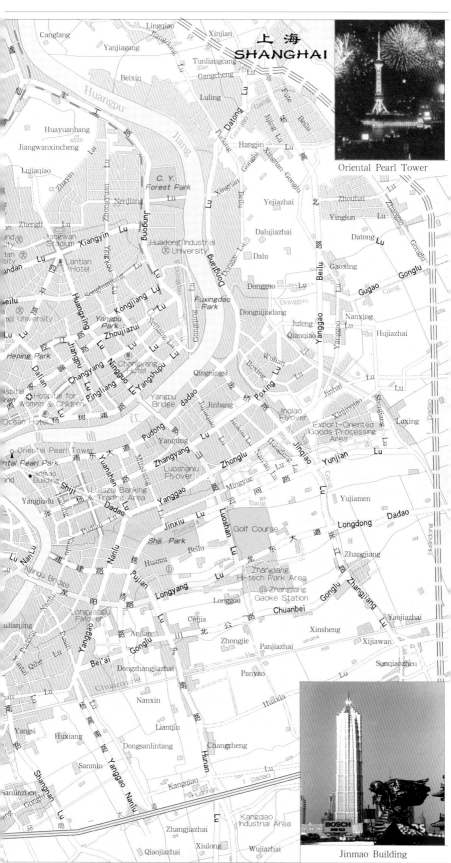

上海
SHANGHAI

Oriental Pearl Tower

Jinmao Building

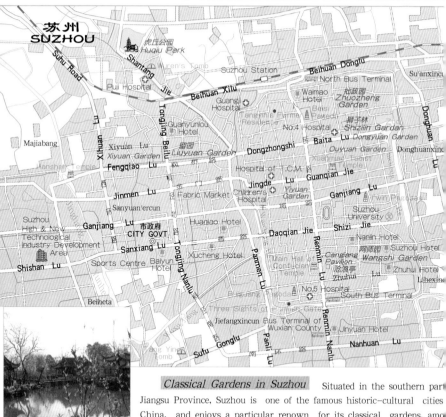

Classical Gardens in Suzhou   Situated in the southern part Jiangsu Province, Suzhou is one of the famous historic–cultural cities China, and enjoys a particular renown for its classical gardens, amo which, Zhuozheng Garden is the most famous. As an ancient garden b in the Ming Dynasty, Zhuozheng Garden enjoys the reputation of one the four most famous gardens in China.

Shouxihu Lake at Shugang

Yangzhou is one of the famous historic–cultural cities in China and possesses many historic sites and scenic spots. Shouxihu Lake is one of them.

Lying in the western suburbs of Yangzhou City, Shouxihu Lake has long been a famous scenic spot since the period of the Six Dynasties.Compared with the Xihu Lake in Hangzhou, it looks more slender and prettier.The lake is more than five km long,looking like a beautiful landscape painting.

50

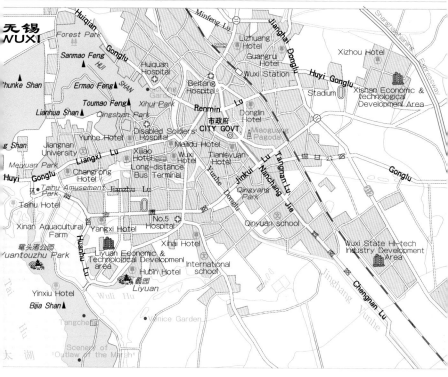

The Vicinity of Taihu Lake

Situated on the shore of Taihu Lake, Wuxi City has a long history and is one of the major tourist cities of Jiangsu Province for its charming scenery. Since ancient times, Wuxi has been a city with prosperous industry and commerce, and is known as a "Minor Shanghai"and a"Pearl on Taihu Lake".

Taihu Lake is located on the southern edge of the Changjiang Delta between Jiangsu and Zhejiang, and is one of the five famous fresh-water lakes in China,occupying a water surface of about 2428 km².

Liyuan   Situated by the side of Lihu Lake, Liyuan is a famous garden of Wuxi City.It consists of the original Liyuan Garden and Yuzhuang(Fishing Village),which were built in 1927 and 1930 respectively and linked by a long corridor.As the story goes, during the Spring and Autumn period,Fan Li,the minister of the Yue State,once boated here companied by Xi Shi.

The garden covers an area of 87 mu, of which water surface occupies 35.3 mu.

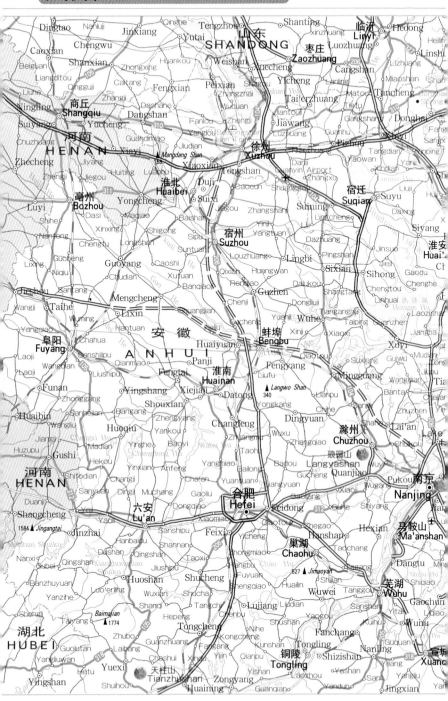

Situated in the lower reaches of the Changjiang River (Yangtze Rive
and bounded by the provinces of Shandong,Zhejiang,Anhui and Shanghai
Jiangsu is a province with wide alluvial plain. There is a intricate network
waterways and a large number of lakes. The well-known Grand Canal
through the entire province from north to south. Most of the province is
than 50 metres above sea level. Area:over 100000 km².

The province enjoys a temperate climate and four distinct seasons, with
moderate rainfall.Its annual mean temperature is 13–16 °C and the annual precipitation is 600–1
mm.With a long history and a rich cultural heritage,Jiangsu possesses a great number of famo

1:2800000

Scale   0   28   56   84 km

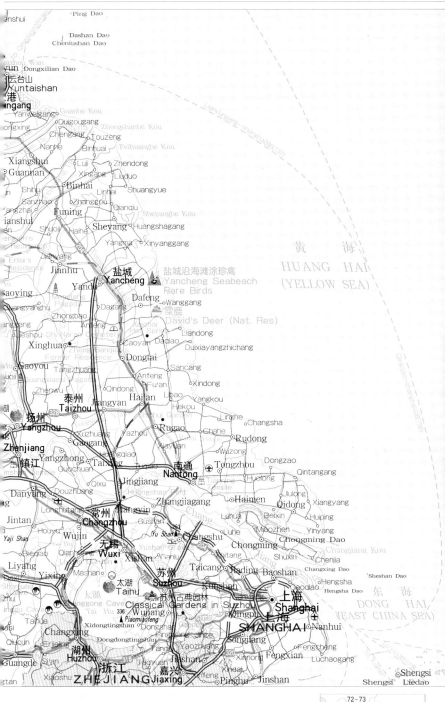

ric-cultural cities,such as Nanjing,Suzhou, Yangzhou, Zhenjiang, Changshu,
hou and Huai'an.In the province, the national major famous scenic areas
Mt.Zhongshan, Taihu Lake, Mt.Yuntai and Shouxihu lake (slender West
),etc.Other famous scenic spots include Sun Yat-sen Mausoleum,the Han
acotta Army in Xuzhou and Ancient Canal, etc.

The province is also famous for its traditional light industrial products and handicrafts, such
mbroidery and straw woven articles in Suzhou,purple pottery in Yixing,clay figuure in Wuxi,
erware in Yangzhou, sandalwood fan and jasmine tea in Suzhou and so on.

53

南京
NANJING

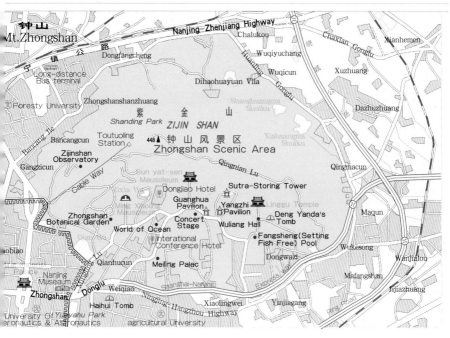

Mt.Zhongshan　Mt.Zhongshan,also known as Mt.Zijin,is the highest peak of Ningzhen Mountains, standing just outside Zhongshanmen Gate of Nanjing City. Mt.Zhongshan is an important scenic area of Nanjing, capital of Jiangsu Province and one of the seven ancient capitals in China's history.It covers an area of 40 km^2 with more than 70 famous scenic sites. The main scenic spots include Heilongtan Pool(Black Dragon Pool),Zixia(Purple Cloud) Cave, Meihua (Plum Blossom) Hill, Taohua (Peach Blossom) Wu, Sun Yat-sen Mausoleum, Ming Xiaoling Mausoleum (Tomb of Zhu Yuanzhang, the first emperor of the Ming Dynasty), Linggu Temple, etc. Sun Yat-sen Mausoleum is located at the southern foot of the west peak of Mt.Zhongshan, which was built in 1929,covering an area of 80000 m^2, and is the most magnificent building in the area.

There are also many other famous scenic spots in Nanjing,such as Mochou Lake,Xuanwu Lake, Yuhuatai Cemetery of Martyrs and Jiming Temple, and the Qinhuai River, etc.

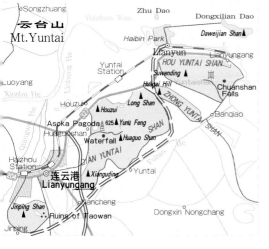

Mt.Yuntai　Situated in the east of Lianyungang City, towering on the coast of the Huanghai Sea (Yellow Sea),Mt.Yuntai is the highest peak of Jiangsu Province. In ancient times, it was originally an island and became a part of the mainland in the early Qing Dynasty. For its sheer peaks, grotesque rocks and clear waters, Mt. Yuntai enjoys the good reputation of being"the wonderland by the Dong-hai Sea".Huaguo Hill boasts the finest scenery in Mt. Yuntai and its Yunü (Jade Maiden) Peak, 625 metres above sea level,is the highest peak in the province.

浙江省 ZHEJIANG PROVINCE

Situated in the coastal area of East China, Zhejiang Province borders Anhui, Jiangsu, Jiangxi, Fujian Provinces and Shanghai Municipality. Area:ov 100000 km².

The province is largely mountainous and has a general slope from sou west to norhteast. Only less than 30 percent of the total area is level land has a rocky and indented coast, forming numerous natural habours.

The climate in Zhejiang is temperate and humid, with an annual m temperature of 15~19℃ and the annual precipitation is 1000~1900 mm.

Zhejiang possesses famous mountains and rivers, so the tourist industry is becoming in easingly developed.Within its boundaries,Mt.Yandang,Mt.Putuo,Mt.Tiantai,Nanxi River,Fuch

Scale 1:2800000

0　28　56　84km

...er-Xin'an River and Xihu Lake(West Lake)are all national major famous ...nic areas, attracting thousands and thousands of tourists both from home ...l abroad, especially, Xihu Scenic Area is among the ten famous scenic ...as in China. There are also other interesting places, such as the world ...ous Qiantang Bore, the famous Taoist mountains-Beishan Hill in Jinhua ...l Mt.Tianmu in Lin'an, etc.

Zhejiang is the home of tea, of which Longjing Tea and Huiming Tea are higly renown-... Besides, silk, bamboo woven articles and embroidery in Hangzhou, orange in Wenzhou,etc, ... all well-known in China.

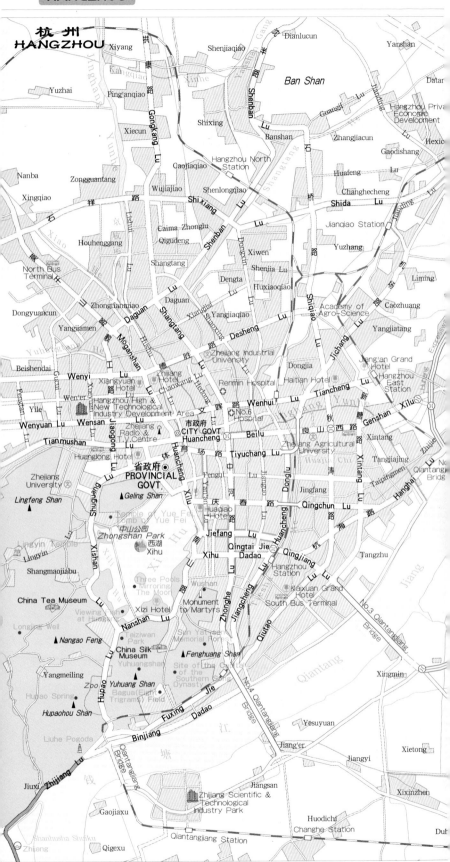

杭 州
HANGZHOU

Xiyang   Shenjiaqiao   Dianlucun   Yanshan

Ban Shan   Datar

Yuzhai   Ping'anqiao   Shixing   Banshan   Zhangjiacun   Hangzhou Priva Economic Development

Nanba   Zongguantang   Shenlongqiao   Huafeng   Changhecheng   Hexic

Xingqiao   Caojiaqiao   Hangzhou North Station   Shida Lu

Houhenggang   Caima Zhonglu   Xiwen   Jianqiao Station

Shangtang   Dengta   Shenjia Lu   Huxiaoqiao   Yuzhang

North Bus Terminal   Zhongtianmiao   Daguan   Yangjiaqiao   Desheng   Academy of Agro-Science   Caozhuang

Dongyuancun   Yangjiamen   Zhejiang Industrial University   Dongjia   Yangjiatang

Beishendai   Wenyi Lu   Xiangyuan Hotel   Renmin Hospital   Haitian Hotel   Jiang'an Grand Hotel

Yile   Hangzhou High & New Technological Industry Development Area   Wenhui   Hangzhou East Station

Wenyuan Lu   Wensan   Zhejiang Radio & T.V. Centre   No.6 Hospital   Beilu   Genshan Xilu

Tianmushan   CITY GOVT. Huancheng   Zhejiang Agricultural University   Xintang

Huanglong Hotel   Tiyuchang Lu   Tangjiajing

Zhejiang University   PROVINCIAL GOVT.   Fengqi   Jingjiang   Qiantang Bridg

Lingfeng Shan   Geling Shan   Huaqiao Hotel   Qingchun   Hanghai

Temple of Yue Fei Tomb of Yue Fei   Jiefang Lu   Qingjiang

Lingyin Temple   Zhongshan Park 西湖 Xihu   Xihu Dadao   Hangzhou Station   Tangzhu

Lingyin   Shangmaojiabu   Three Pools Mirroring The Moon   Wushan   Kaixuan Grand Hotel South Bus Terminal

China Tea Museum   Xizi Hotel   Monument to Martyrs   No.3 Qiantangjiang

Longjing Well   Nanshan   Sun Yat-sen Memorial Hall   Xingmin

Nangao Feng   China Silk Museum   Fenghuang Shan   Qiantang

Yangmeiling   Yuhuang Shan   Site of the Capital of the Southern Dynasty

Zoo   Bagua(Eight Trigrams) Field   Yesuyuan

Hupao Spring   Hupaohou Shan   Fuxing Dadao   Jiang'er

Liuhe Pagoda   Binjiang   Xietong

Jiuxi Zhijiang Lu   Qiantangjiang Bridge   Jiangsan   Xixinzhen

Zhejiang Scientific & Technological Industry Park   Huodichi   Dub

Gaojiaxu   Changhe Station

Shantusha Shunku Zhijiang   Qigexu   Qiantangjiang Station

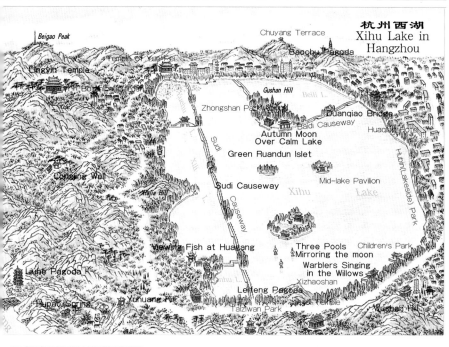

Xihu Lake in Hangzhou　Hangzhou,capital of Zhejiang Province,enjoys good fame for its ﹍hu (West Lake) Scenic Area lying to the west of city proper. Among more than 30 lakes named ﹍er "Xi Hu", the Xihu Lake in Hangzhou is the most fascinating.

The Xihu Lake occupies an area of more than 6 km^2 and is 15 km in circumference,with many ﹍nic spots and historic sites scattered all over the scenic area.

Fuchun R.–xin'an R.

This scenic area starts ﹍om Hangzhou in the east ﹍aches Huangshan City in ﹍e west. It is famous for ﹍e picturesque scenes along ﹍e rivers. The main scenic ﹍ots and historic sites are ﹍aolin Cave in Tonglu, ﹍anziling Fishing Platform, ﹍ngjun Hill, Hulu Falls, ﹍win Pagodas in Meicheng ﹍d Qiandao(thousand islets) ﹍ake, etc, among them, ﹍andao Lake is the largest ﹍ scale.

Mt.Putuo　Situated within Zhoushan Islands, Mt. Putuo is one of the four famous Buddhist mountains in China. It is actually a small island of Zhoushan Islands,covering an area of 12.5 km^2,with more than 300 temples,among which Puji,Fayu and Huiji Temples are the most famous. The main scenic spots include Qianbusha Beach, Chaoyang Cave, Fanyin Cave, South Heavenly Gate and West Heavenly Gate, etc.

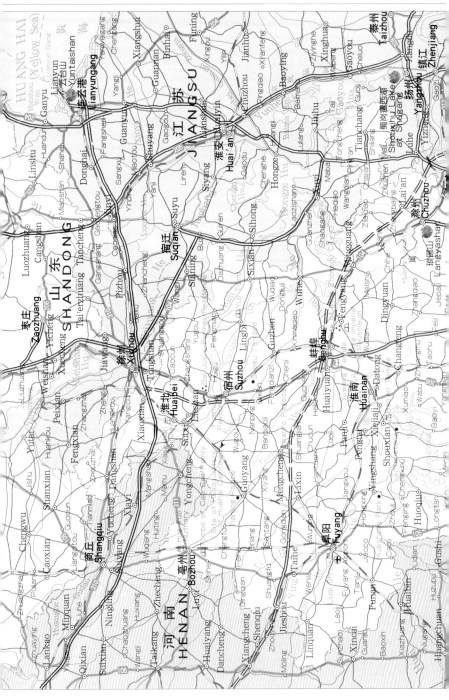

Lying in the lower reaches of the Changjiang (Yangtze) River and central part of East China, Anhui is bounded by Jiangsu and Zhejiang the east, Hunan and Hubei on the west, Jiangxi on the south and Shandong the north, with the Changjiang River and the Huaihe River flowing throu it. Area: over 130000 km².

Anhui has an uneven terrain. Its northern portion is occupied by No China Plain, while its southern and western parts are mountainous, with series of beautiful mountains and hills.

The province enjoys a temperate and humid monsoon climate characterized by distinct fo

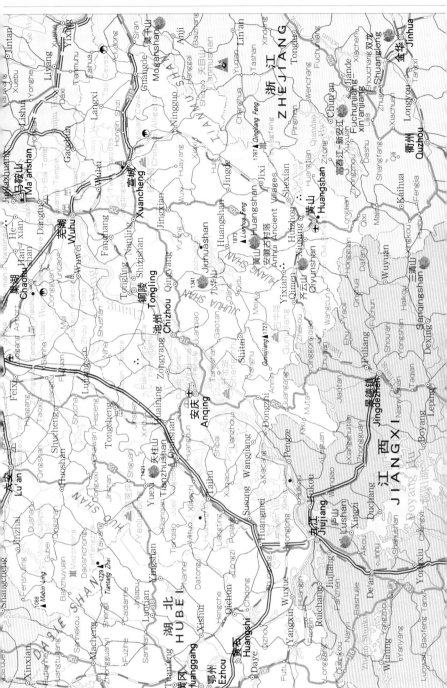

ons. The annual mean temperature is 14-17 ℃ and the annual precipita-

is 770-1700 mm.

Anhui possesses a long-standing historical civilization and picturesque

eries. The national major famous scenic areas include Mt. Huangshan, Mt.

zhu, Mt. Jiuhua and Mt. Langya.Besides,the local-style dwelling hou-

have won the reputation of "An Epitome of Oriental Civilization". The ancient Villages of Xidi

Hongcun have been included in The World Heritages.

The specialities in Anhui are famous in China. Black tea in Qimen, green tea in Huangshan, the

tional handicrafts and the four treasures of study, etc, all enjoy good fame in the country.

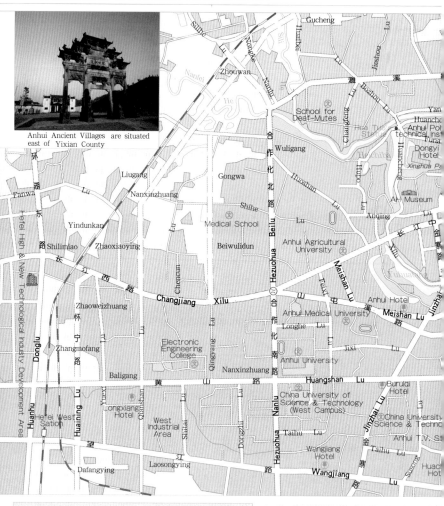

Anhui Ancient Villages are situated east of Yixian County

九华山
Mt. Jiuhua

Mt. Jiuhua Standing to the south west of Qingyang County, Mt. Jiuhua is one of the four sacred Buddhist mountains China, covering more than 100 km². Amor the 99 peaks in the mountain, 9 peaks su as Tiantai, Lianhua, Tianzhu, Shiwan etc, are the most magnificent. The highe Shiwang Peak has an elevation of 13 metres above sea level.

Mt. Jiuhua possesses clear rivers, beauti waterfalls, bizarre rocks, caves, green pin and bamboos. It also has famous ancier temples and other historic sites. Now, ther are still 78 ancient temples, such as Huac eng Temple, Huiju Temple and Baisu Palace, etc., among which, Huacheng Templ is one of the main ancient temples in China. Therefore, it has been known as "The first mountain in Southeast China".

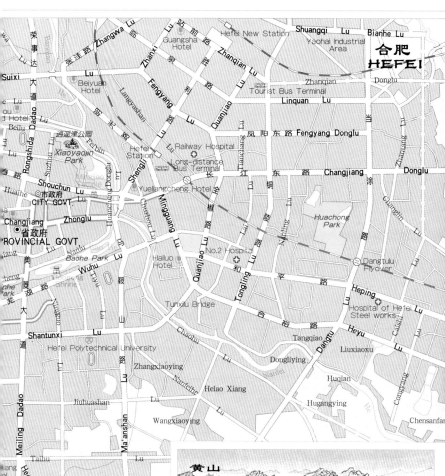

Mt. Huangshan Located in the southern part of Anhui Province, Mt. Huangshan is one of the famous scenic areas in China. It was once called Yishan Mountain in the Qin Dynasty. The scenic area, covering more than 150 km^2, possesses many fascinating scenes, and was included in the List of World Heritages by UNESCO in 1990.

Mt.Huangshan has received high praise for its wonderful mountain scenery: old-shaped pines, grotesque rocks, seas of clouds and hot springs. There are 72 famous sheer peaks with different heights and shapes, and the rocks of grotesque shapes resemble various things that you can imagine. Xu Xiake,a noted traveller and geographer in the Ming Dynasty, once exclaimed, "Mt.Huangshan has no equal. Once on top, one would fine no other match. This is the acme."

福建省　FUJIAN PROVINCE

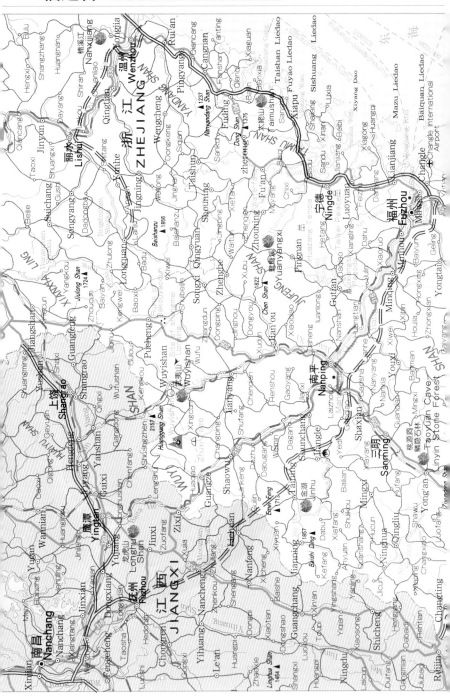

Situated in the southeastern coast of China , Fujian Province Borders
Zhejiang,Jiangxi,Guangdong Provinces and faces Taiwan across the Strait.Ar
over 120000 km².

　　The province is mountainous and only the area along the coast is occu
by plains. Mountainous areas and hilly lands make up 80% of its total a

　　Fujian enjoys a subtropic climate , characterized by hot summer but c
winter. The annual mean temperature is 17~22℃ , and the annual rainfal
1100~2000mm. It has a frost-free Period of 240~300 days in a year.

　　The province is rich in tourist resources and famous for its picturesque sceneries. It posse

re than 40 famous scenic spots and over 40 major historic and cultural
s under state protection. The national major famous scenic areas include
Wuyi, Mt.Taimu,Mt.Qingyuan, Gulangyu-Wanshishan, Taoyuan Cave,
yin Stone Forest , Yuanyang Brook , Mt. Guanzhi and Jinhu Lake in
ining. Others,such as the "Eighteen sights in Gushan" and the "Thirty-

Wonderful Views in Wushan Hill" are also the attractive tourist sites.

Fujian is famous for its traditional handicraft articles , such as bodiless lacquerware in Fu-
ou, stone carving in Shoushan, bamboo woven articles in Anxi, shell carving in Pingtan, etc,
ecially, the narcissus in Zhangzhou enjoys good fame throughout the country.

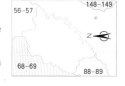

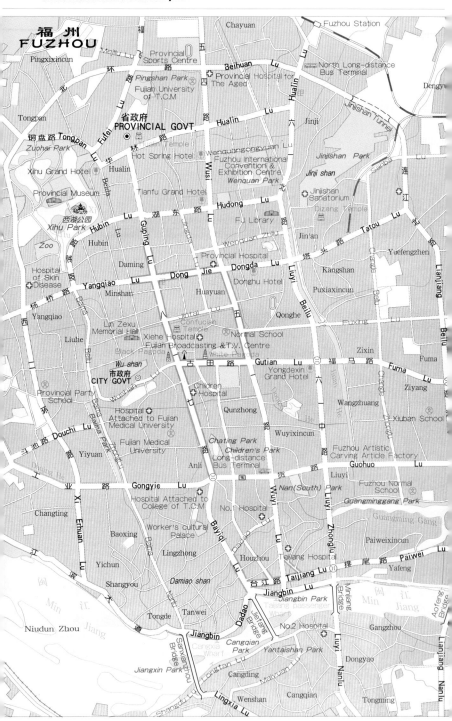

福州
FUZHOU

Mt.Wuyi Situated 15 km south of Wuyishan City, Mt.Wu covers an area of about 60 km², with streams and valleys snak their ways through the mountains, and is known as " the m beautiful mountain in Southeast China".

Mt.Wuyi boasts fascinating 36 peaks, 9 caves, 99 distinguishe rocks and 108 scenic spots, and its scenery is an integration the wonder of Mt. Huangshan, the elegance of Guilin, the beau of Xihu Lake in Hangzhou and the grandeur of Mt.Taishan.It also famous for its cultural actvities in China's history.

厦门
XIAMEN

Jiamei
Library
Hospital
Aquatic Products School
Aoyuan Garden
Jiageng Tomb

Xiamen North Station
Xiamen West Station
Gaoqi International Airport
Fangzhong
Lu

Xun
Jiang
Daliao Shuiku
Lingxia

Zhaishang
Andou
Linhou
Xfanhou
Xfanhou

Subtropic Plants Research Institute
Xinghu
Huoju High-tech Industry Area
Fanghu
Xiazhong

Yuehua Hotel
Huli
Dadao
Xiaodongshan
Jinhu
Lu
Dongliu

Paitou
Haitian Wharf
Yibin
Lu
Lu

Nanshan
Technial School
Xianyue Shan
Xiandong Shan
Xianyue Hospital
Heshan Hospital
Xiangdian

Haicang Bridge
Yuhou
Heshan High School

Aquatic Products School
Liuling
Lushan Hotel
Long shan
Dongfang Shan

市政府
CITY GOVT
Hubing
Nanhu Park
Daitou
Commercial School
Banlanshan Substation
Lu

Long-distance Bus Terminal
Zhongshan Hospital
Nanlu
Jinghua Hotel
Institute of Geological Engineeing Prospecting
Wenxing

Hualian Hotel
Hubing Hotel
Xiahe
Xiamen Station
Southeast Asia Hotel
Dongshan Shuiku

Bailu Hotel
Biyan Shan
Yunding Crag

Zhongshan Park
Wanshishan
Dongping Shan
Guanying Shan
Maohou Shuiku

Huli Crag
Hongshan Park
园林植物园
Yuanlin Botanical Garden
Taiping Shan
Houcuo Shan
Shangli Shuiku
Maohou

Huangliadu Park
Ganlu Temple
Bishan Temple
Overseas Chinese Museum
Zheng Chenggong Statue
Nanputuo Temple
Shi Shan
Jinshanzhai Shan
Tatou

LANGYU
Xiamen University
Oceanological Institute
Xibian
Zeng Shan

Hulishan Bathing Beach
Xiamen
Gang
厦门港

Gulangyu Situated to the southwest of Xiamen City, Gulangyu is a small island facing Xiamen across a narrow strait. It is covered by luxuriant green trees, and many western style villas are scattered over the island,forming a beautiful sight.Riguang(Sunlight) Crag is the highest peak of the island and an ideal spot of viewing Xiamen City and the seascape.

Situated on the south bank in the middle reaches of the Changjiang (Ya tze)River, Jiangxi is bounded by Zhejiang, Fujian, Anhui, Hubei, Hunan and Guangdong Provinces. Area: over 160000 km².

The province is surrounded on three sides by mountains and hills, w hilly lands occupying its central part and a vast plain lying on the north part. The five rivers—Ganjiang River, Xinjiang River, Pojiang River, Xiushu River and Fuhe River, all drain into the Poyang Lake, the largest fre water lake in China.

Jiangxi enjoys a subtropic humid monsoon climate.The annual mean temperature is 16−20° The annual average rainfall is 1200−1900 mm.

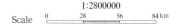

1:2800000

Scale 0   28   56   84 km

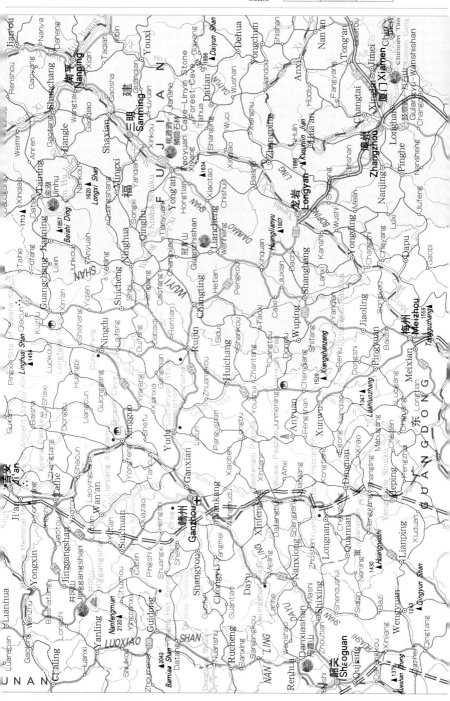

...he province possesses green mountains and clear waters. Mt.Lushan,Mt. ...ang and Mt.Longhu are all national major famous scenic areas,especially ...Lushan Scenic Area is a summer resort renowned both at home and ...d. There are also many other famous tourist attractions, like Longgong ...on Palace) Cave with fantastic scenery. Jiangxi is also a province with ...utionary tradition, where the August 1 Nanchang Uprising had taken place.

...Porcelain and porcelain engravings are the most famous local products in Jingdezhen. Bamboo ...n articles in Yanshan,fire crackers in Wanzai, fireworks in Pingxiang, also enjoy good fame ...hina. The traditional local products—Yunwu tea of Lushan,green tea of Wuyuan and bamboo ...ts in Mt.Jinggang,etc,are all famous.

Mt.Jinggang Situated in the bor area between Jiangxi and Hunan,Mt.Jinggan is not only a famous revolutionary site China, but also a major famous scenic are with more than twenty scenic spots.

In October 1927,Mao Zedong led the ar organized during the Autumn Uprising to Jinggang Mountain and established the f revolutionary base area of the Chinese Co munist Party. A long period of revolutiona struggle of the Red Army led by the Chin Communist Party has left a great number revolutionary sites.

The Jinggang Mountain also possesses ma magnificent natural sceneries, for example, t waterfalls on the Wushen River enjoy g fame, among which, Bailongtan Waterfall ha a drop of 82 metres, presenting a magnifice sight.

Mt.Lushan Located to the south of Jiujiang City,Mt.Lushan is the best-known scenic area and summer resort, with the Poyang Lake lying to its east and the Changjiang(Yangtze)River flowing by its north.It covers an area of 394 km^2.

Mt. Lushan possesses beautiful natural sceneries. Towering peaks, changeable sea of clouds,numerous gurgling springs and waterfalls cascading down the precipitous cliffs form a fascinating scenery. The main scenic spots include Wulao Peak, Hanpokou Archway, Hanyang Peak, Lulin Lake, Sanbao (Three Treasure) Trees, Ruqin Lake, Xianren Cave and Botanical Garden, etc. Mt. Lushan attracts tourists also for its being always shrouded in swirling mist and clouds.

It is also famous for its ancient temples. Donglin Temple, Xilin Temple and Dalin Temple are the three famous temples.

70

南昌
NANCHANG

Nitan

Yangzi Zhou

Gan Jiang

赣江

Ganliang Bridge

Yangzizhou Lu

Tongziqiao

Xincun

Liujia

Huabiao

Qingshanhu Scenic Area

Qingshan Hu

Qingshanhu Amusement Park

Changxiangdengjia

Kangshan Hotel

Fuzhou

Dongjiayao

Luojiafang

No.8 Hospital

Commercial School

Dongjiayao

Qingshan Lu

Shishan Lu

Erqi

Dadu

Renmin Hospital

Wuwei

a Zhou

Bridge Binjiang

Dieshan

Yangming Hotel

Yongwai

Xiushi Hu

Xiongjijia

Weijia

Xutaihua

Yangjiafang

Nanchang University
南昌大学

Huoju Dajie

Dongju

Hubin

Jiangxi Medical College

Yangming Lu

Experiment Middle School

Zhengjie

Yinjiadun

Hongdu Dadao

Nanjing

Museum

Changzheng

Jiangxi Hotel

Jiangxi Medical College

Fuzhou

Qingshanhu Hotel

Zoo

Renmin Park

Stadium

Huaxin Hotel

Dieshan

Bayi Park

Jiangxi Hotel

Changzheng

Provincial Gymnasium

Lu

CITY GOVT.
市政府

Minde

大

Zhongshan

Aug.1 Uprising Memorial Hall

Xi Hu

Uprising

Lu

道

PROVINCIAL GOVT.
省政府

北京路

Jiangxi Normal University

Agricultural Edifice

Beijing Lu

Jinghai Shopping Center

Ruziting Park

Jiaotong Hotel

Library

Erqi

Jiangxi T.V. Station

Xiaopengjia

No.1 Middle School

Xinweicun

洪

Jicheng Hotel

Long-distance Bus Terminal

Sanduwancun

Tangxiawancun

Hufang

Nanchang Hotel

Zhanqian Xilu

Bayi Hotel

大

Wanjia

No.3 Hospital

Jun'an Edifice

Shengjin Pagoda

Zhanqian Lu

Nanchang Station

Xiecun

Wucun

Taziqiaowangjia

Shanghai-luxincun

Hongcheng Lu

Qingyun Hotel

解放西路

Lijiazhuang

Jiefang Xilu

Zhengjia

Taziqiao

Taohua

Greatwall Hotel

Lengshang-wanjia

Lengshang-xiongjia

Luobo zhou

Jianshe Bridge

Jianshe Xilu

Jianshe Lu

Xujiafang

Maoxia

Shitingzixia

Yangjiatai

Zhuanwanli

Qingyun Waterworks

Xujiafang

Ganjiang Hotel

Qianli

Jiangxi Chengxin Clothing College

Jingshancun

Xinxiqiao

Jinggangshan Dadao

Hefang Xilu

Siwangtang

Sandian Xilu

Sanjiadian

Jiangxi Clothing College

Shizikou

No.13 Middle School

Xiayao

Provincial Machine Industry School

Qingyunpu Middle School

Wanxixincun

Jiangling Automobile Group Pota

Yingbin Dadao

Nanfan Lu

Huangxicun

gwang Pavilion is standing by the
ang River south of Nanchang City

山东省 SHANDONG PROVINCE

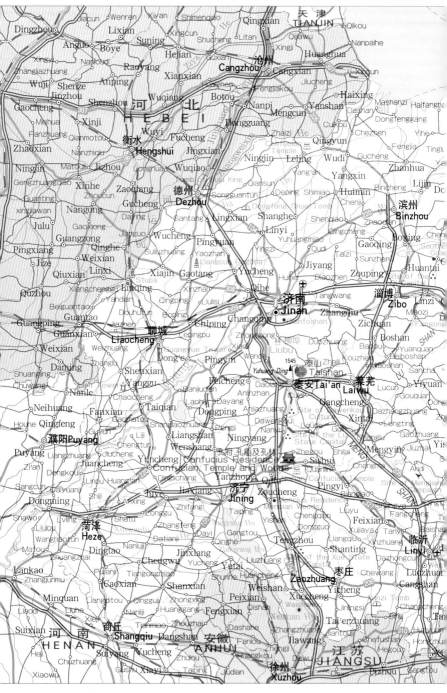

Lying in the lower reaches of the Huanghe River(Yellow River), Shand
borders on Hebei, Henan, Anhui and Jiangsu Provinces. Area: over 156000 k

Shandong is dominated by plains and hilly lands. Its central part is hig
than the surrounding areas, and about 20 percent of its land is occupied
mountainous and hilly areas. Mt.Taishan, Mt.Mengshan, Mt.Laoshan, Mt.I
shan, Mt.Yishan and Mt.Culai are the main mountains of the province, am
them, Mt.Taishan is the highest.

The Province has a temperate monsoon climate. The annual mean tempe
ture is 11-14°C, and the annual precipitation is 550-950 mm.

Shandong is one of the birthplaces of the ancient Chinese civilization and has a recorded h

Scale 1:2800000

of 4000 years.

It possesses famous sceneries with hills and waters,and numerous histo-
sites.Mt.Taishan,Mt.Laoshan in Qingdao,and the seasides in   the eastern
stal area,are all national major famous scenic areas,in which,Mt.Taishan
been listed in the World Natural and Cultural Heritages by UNESCO in
. Other scenic spots include Confucian Temple, Confucius Residence and Confucian Woods in
ı and Penlai Pavilion in Penglai City, etc.

The main local products include clocks and watches in Yantai,Pottery and porceliain in Zibo,
s in Weifang, etc. Besides, Laiyang pear, Yantai apple, Leling   date and Jimo grape are all
ous in China, and Qingdao beer, however, is world-famous.

济南
Jinan

菫莱阁
Penglai Pavilion

Penglai Pavilion Standing on the top of Danya hill north of Penglai City, Penglai Pavilion is a famous tourist site of Shandong Province. According to legend, Penglai was known as one of the three fairy mountains on the sea. The Pavilion,built in the Northern Song Dynasty, was extended in the Ming Dynasty and rebuilt in the Qing Dynasty, with Sanqing Hall,Lizhu Hall, Tianhou Palace and Longwang (Dragon King) Palace standing to its south.

Penglai Pavilion has long been the place where the men of letters and refined scholars often visited.

QINGDAO Mt.Laoshan

崂山
Laoshan

Huilou Palace
Laoding Peak
Nationaidini Peak
Huayan Temple
Taiping Palace
Stone Old Man
Taiping Palace
Dafu Island
HUANG HAI
(YELLOW SEA)
Laogong Island

Mt. Laoshan   Situated 35 km east of Qingdao City, Mt. Laoshan is a national major scenic area with towering Peaks, high cliffs, deep and serene ancient caves, clear springs and waterfalls. It has a long history and humid climate, with a large number of Taoist temples built in past dynasties. Mt. Laoshan is an ideal summer resort and famous scenic area.

青岛
QINGDAO

Zunyi Lu
Cuijiagou
Shimei'an
Luoquanjian
Dazaoyuan
Huanghuading
Yandunshan Park
Loushan Park
Tangshan Lu
Cangqing Park
Xinghua Lu
Laohu Shan
Cangkou Station
Wenchangge
No.3 Renmin Hospital
Cangkou Bus Terminal
Zhenhua
Xiaowengcun
Dacun
Jingkou
Licun
Dongnianshan
Shaoshan Lu
Xincun
Jiaozhou Wan
Zhengzhou Lu
Yanjiashan
Nanlu
Tanghe Lu
NanLu
Luoyang Lu
Qingfang Hospital
Kaiping
Heya
Hedong
Gu Shan
Chongqing
Hexi
Xihangezhuang
Hudaocun
Yangjiaqun
Xintian Hotel
Ruichang
Jinhua
Hi-Tech. Industry Park Area
Yichang Lu
Zhuangi Hotel
Beilingshan Park
Shuang Shan
Jiadingshan Park
Tailu
Hemashi
Xilu
Sifang Station
Long-distance Bus Terminal
Fuzhou Lu
Liao yang
Renmin
Ha'erbin
Wenhua Park
Changchun
Xinxing Hotel
Dagang
Dunhua
Nanjing
Shaoxing
Beilu
Dagang Station
Huilu Hotel
Qingning Lu
Children's Palace
Shandong
Ningxia
Fu Shan
Fushan Forest Park
City Hospital
Yan'an Lu
Kang Youwei's Tomb
Ningxia
Overseas Chinese resturant
Jiaozhou Lu
Guanxiangshan Park
Qingdaoshan Park
Zhongshan Park
CITY GOVT
市政府
Qingdao University
am Ferry
Qingdao Station
Dongfang Hotel
Huanghai Resturant
Botanical Garden
Donghai
Xinjiazhuang
Xianggang
Yan'erdao Hotel
Sichuan Lu
Zhangh
Huanhai Hotel
Haibin Park
Huilan Pavilion
Xiling
Fushansun Kou
Haitian Hotel
Xiaoqingdao Park
Huiquan Dynasty Hotel
NO.3 Bathing Beach
Yan'er Dao
Mai Dao
Tuandao Wan
Badaguan Scenic Spot
Huiquan Jiao
Taiping Jiao
HUANG HAI
(YELLOW SEA)
Tuan Dao

Mt. Taishan Toweri
in the central part of Shandor
Province, Mt.Taishan, with i
elevation of 1545 metres abo
sea level, is the first of China
five sacred mountains and o
of the national major famou
scenic areas. In 1987, Mt.Taisha
was listed in the World Natur
and Cultural Heritages t
UNESCO.

In history, emperors ar
many scholars stepped on th
mountain to view its magnif
cent scenery, having left qui
a many famous poems ar
inscriptions.

The main scenic spots ar
Wangmu (Heavenly Mother
Pool, Doumu Palace, Jingsl
(Sutra Rock) Valley, Heilor
(Black Dragon)Pool,Shanzi(Fa
-shaped)cliff,Changshou(Longevity)Bridge.Daimiao Templo
situated in Tai'an City at th
southern foot of the mountair
was first built in the Han Dy
nasty, and large-scale addi-
tions were made during th
Tang and Song Dynasties.
is a key cultural heritag
under state protection.

Qufu During the Spring and Autumn period, Qufu was the capital of the Lu State and the birthpalce of the world-famous thinker Confucius. It possesses abundance of cultural relics and historic sites, of which, Confucian Temple, Confucius Residance and Confucian Woods are the most famous. Confucian Temple is one of the three palatial architectures in China, which houses a large number of steles and other cultural relics. Confucius Residence covers 120000 sq. metres and is a magnificent mansion only next to imperial palace of the Ming or Qing Dynasties in scale.

Confucian Woods, the cemetery for Confucius and his descendants, has a history of over 2300 years, covering more than 200 hectares.

Mt.Songshan Located in the northwest of Dengfeng County and reputed as the Central Sacred Mountain among China's five sacred mountains, Mt. Songshan Stretches more than 60 km across from east to west. It consists of two mountains—Taishi and Shaoshi,with 36 peaks altogether.

Longmen Grottoes Located 13 km south of Luoyang City, Longmen Grottoes constitute one of the four most famous treasure houses of grotto art in China, housing more than 100000 Buddha statues,of which the highest is more than 17 metres high.

龙门石窟
Longmen Grottoes

77

河南省　HENAN PROVINCE

Situated in the central part of China, Henan Province is bounded by H
Shandong, Anhui, Shanxi, Shaanxi and Hubei, and separated into two une
parts by the Huanghe River(Yellow River), Area:over 167000 km^2.

The province is divided topographically into two parts: the western h
lands and the eastern plain.

Henan has a temperate continental monsoon climate, with a long and
winter and a hot and rainy summer. The annual mean temperature is 13−
and the annual precipitation is 600−1200 mm.

The province has a long history and a developed culture. As early as 5−6 thousands y
ago, it had the Peiligang culture and Yangshao culture, and enjoys the reputation of "the Crad

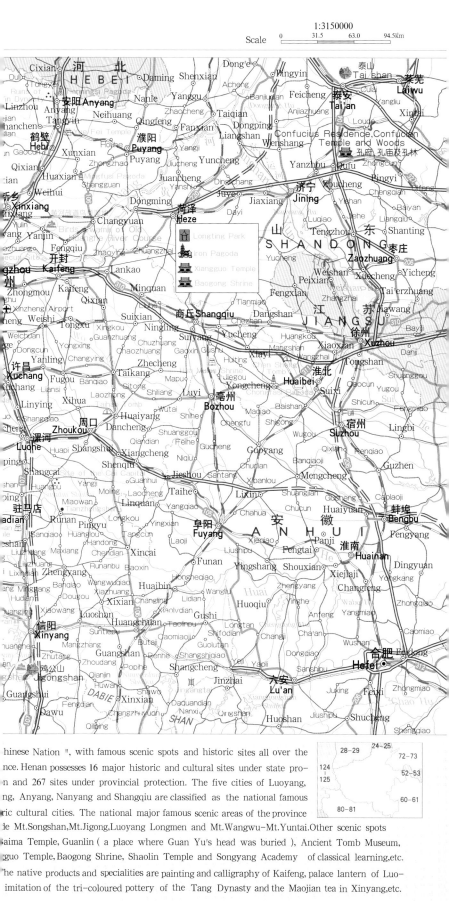

hinese Nation ", with famous scenic spots and historic sites all over the ... nce. Henan possesses 16 major historic and cultural sites under state pro- ... n and 267 sites under provincial protection. The five cities of Luoyang, ... ng, Anyang, Nanyang and Shangqiu are classified as the national famous ... ric cultural cities. The national major famous scenic areas of the province ... ie Mt.Songshan,Mt.Jigong,Luoyang Longmen and Mt.Wangwu-Mt.Yuntai.Other scenic spots ... aima Temple, Guanlin (a place where Guan Yu's head was buried), Ancient Tomb Museum, ... guo Temple, Baogong Shrine, Shaolin Temple and Songyang Academy of classical learning,etc. ...

he native products and specialities are painting and calligraphy of Kaifeng, palace lantern of Luo- ... imitation of the tri-coloured pottery of the Tang Dynasty and the Maojian tea in Xinyang,etc.

Situated in the middle reaches of the Changjiang(Yangtze)River and n
of Dongting Lake, Hubei Province borders on Anhui, Jiangxi, Hunan, Shaa
Provinces and Chongqing Municipality. Area:more than 180000 km².

The province, a part of the middle basin of the Changjiang River
surrounded by mountains on three sides. Mountainous areas and hilly la
make up 70% of its total land.

Hubei enjoys a subtropic monsoon climate, with abundant rainfall an
long frost-free period.The annual mean temperature is 13-18C°, and the an
rainfall is 750-1600 mm.

The province has a long history and developed culture, and is one of the birthplaces of

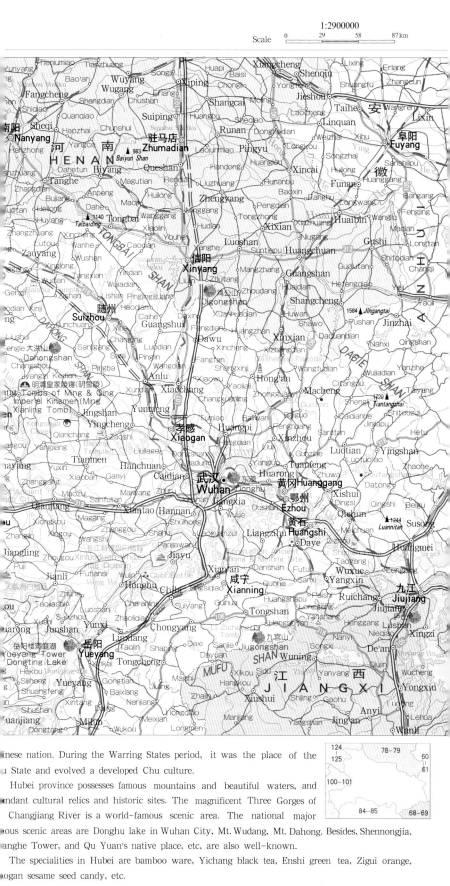

1:2900000
Scale

0   29   58   87km

...inese nation. During the Warring States period, it was the place of the
... State and evolved a developed Chu culture.

　　Hubei province possesses famous mountains and beautiful waters, and
...ndant cultural relics and historic sites. The magnificent Three Gorges of
... Changjiang River is a world-famous scenic area. The national major
...ous scenic areas are Donghu lake in Wuhan City, Mt. Wudang, Mt. Dahong. Besides, Shennongjia,
...anghe Tower, and Qu Yuan's native place, etc, are also well-known.

　　The specialities in Hubei are bamboo ware, Yichang black tea, Enshi green tea, Zigui orange,
...ogan sesame seed candy, etc.

Mt. Wudang Standing southwest of Danjiangkou City, Mt. Wudang is one of the famous mountains to the Taoists. It is 400 km in circumference and has such natural sceneries as 72 peaks, 24 ravines, 11 caves, 9 springs, 3 pools, 9 wells, 10 rocks and 9 terraces. The ancient architecture complex is also famous in China and abroad, including 8 palaces, 2 Taoist temples, 36 nunneries, 72 temples, 39 bridges and 12 pavilions. Since the Tang Dynasty. Mt. Wudang has become a centre of Taoism and a famous scenic area. It had a period of great prosperity in the Ming

82

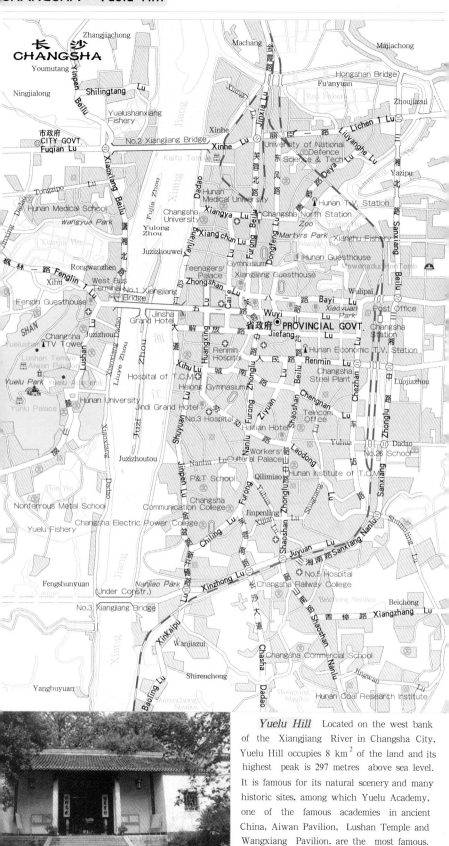

Yuelu Hill Located on the west bank of the Xiangjiang River in Changsha City, Yuelu Hill occupies 8 km² of the land and its highest peak is 297 metres above sea level. It is famous for its natural scenery and many historic sites, among which Yuelu Academy, one of the famous academies in ancient China, Aiwan Pavilion, Lushan Temple and Wangxiang Pavilion, are the most famous. Besides, Yuelu Palace is also a scenic spot.

湖南省 HUNAN PROVINCE

Lying on the south bank in the middle reaches of the Changjiang (Yan
tze)River,the province borders on Jiangxi,Guizhou,Hubei,Guangxi and Chon
qing Municipality. The Changjiang River flows through its northern part an
brings a large amount of water into the Dongting Lake.Area:over 210000km²

Hunan province is surrounded by the uplands in the west,south and ea
which fall steadily toward the plain of the Dongting Lake in the nor
Mountainous areas and hilly lands consitute 80% of the total area.

It enjoys a subtropic humid monsoon climate with distinct four seaso
The annual mean temperature is 15−18.5℃ and the annual rainfall is 1300−1800mm.

Hunan has a long history and a great number of cultural relics, historic sites and a beaut
scenery of lakes and mountains. The well−known scenic areas, such as Mt.Hengshan, Wulir

Yueyang Tower,Dongting Lake and Shaoshan—the home village of Mao
...g, are all the national major famous scenic areas,among which Wuling-
... Scenic Area was included in the World Heritages by UNESCO. Besides,
...ror Yan's Mausoleum, Yuelu Academy—one of the four famous academies
... e Song Dynasty,and Taohuayuan,etc,are all quite familiar to the visitors.
...n is also one of the birthplaces of the new democratic revolution of China, therefore, the
...r residences of Mao Zedong, Liu Shaoqi and the sites of the Autumn Uprising and Pingjiang
...ing have long been the famous tourist sites.

The output of lotus seeds ranks the first in China, while the output of tea and orange ranks
...econd. "Silver needle" tea in Junshan,   Maojian green tea in Dayong, Yinfeng green tea in
...gsha, and the porcelain in Liling are all famous local products.

Mt.Hengshan　Wulingyuan

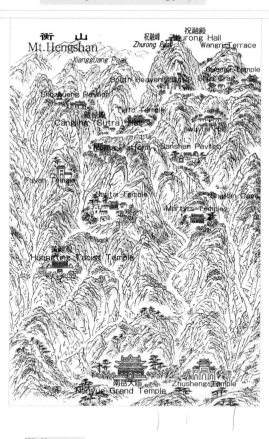

Mt.Hengshan Situated in the ce part of Hunan Province, Mt.Hengshan known as the Southern Sacred Mour one of the five great mountains in Ch and has been praised as "the first fo beauty among the five famous mounta It boasts beautiful natural sceneries, peaks rising one upon another. Among 72 towering peaks, Zhurong Peak is highest, rising to 1290 metres above level.

Mt. Hengshan has ancient cultural (gins. According to historical records, th were nine emperors of the past dyna visiting Mt. Hengshan and many scho also made their tours of the mour having left many inscriptions and po The main scenic spots include Grand Na Temple,Zhusheng Temple,Huangting Tac Temple, Nantai Temple, Sutra Hall Yehou Academy,the earliest academy w preserved.

Wulingyuan Located in Zhangjiajie City, Wulingyuan Scenic Area covers an area of 396 kn consisting of Zhangjiajie National Forest Park, Suoxiyu Scenic Spot and Tianzishan Nature Reserve The spectacular quartz−sandstone landform is noted for its clusters of peaks in wonderful shapes w clear streams flowing through them.

Wulingyuan has a forest coverage of 85% and vegetation coverage of 99%,with abundance of wildli Zhangjiajie National Forest Park is the first one established in China.Famous scenic spots are Jinb (Gold Whip)Crag, Huangshi(Yellow Lion)Crag, Fuqi(Husband&Wife)Crag and Shadaogou, etc. Tourists both from home and abroad praise Zhangjiajie as "a pearl in the remote mountains" or "a scenic ar of the first class in the world".

Situated in the southern part of China on the Nanhai Sea (South Ch
Sea), the province borders on Jiangxi, Hunan, Fujian and Guangxi, and i
separated from Hainan Province by the Qiongzhou Strait. Area:about 1800
km².

Guangdong comprises plains, tablelands,hilly lands and mountainous are
Smooth,low hills cover about 70% of the total land.It has the longest coastl
and a great number of islands.

The province enjoys a tropic and subtropic climate,with abundant rainfall. The annual me
temperature is over 19℃, and the annual rainfall is approximately 1500−2000 mm.

Guangdong boasts many charming sceneries. Xinghu Lake in Zhaoqing, and Mt. Danxia

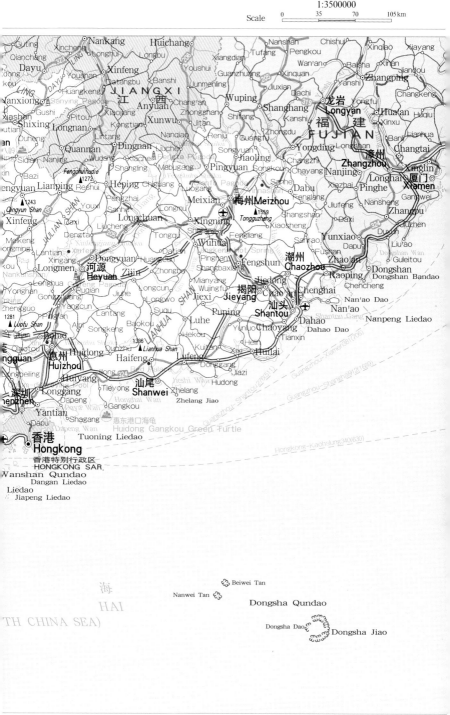

hua are the national major famous scenic areas.Mt. Dinghu in Zhaoqing,

xiu Hill,Qinghui Garden in Shunde,Keyuan Garden in Dongguan,Liang-

n Garden in Foshan, the newly built miniature landscape "Splendid

na" and "China Folk Culture Villages" in Shenzhen,etc,are all attractive

es. Dr.Sun Yat-sen Memorial Hall in Guangzhou, the former residences

he celebrities in modern times, important sites and cemeteries are also well-known tourist spots.

Guangdong is the hometown of tropical and subtropical fruits and teas, such as banana in

gguan,orange in Chaozhou,lychee in Zengcheng and black tea in Yingde,etc.The handicraft arti-

, for example, embroidery, drawnwork, artistic porcelain,ivory carving,etc, are famous in China.

ides, Guangdong cuisine is also well-known both at home and abroad.

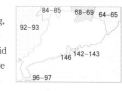

89

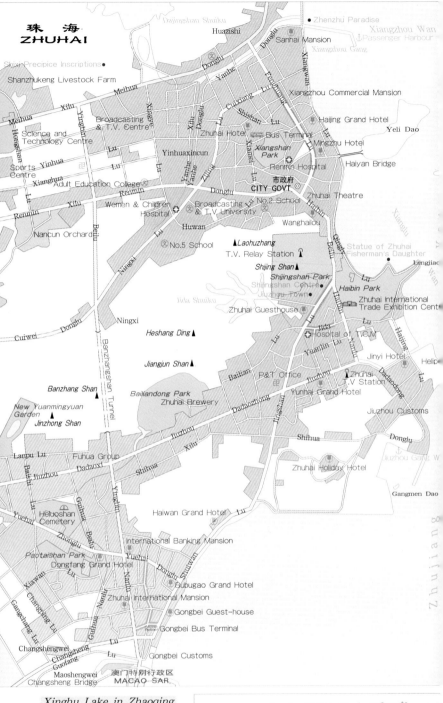

珠海
ZHUHAI

Xinghu Lake in Zhaoqing

Situated in Zhaoqing City, Xinghu Lake, also called Qixingyan(Seven-star Crags）, is a national famous scenic area, dotted with seven hills looking like seven stars, occupying 8.2 km² of land. It is noted for its fascinating scenery and has won the fame of "an integration of the beauty of the hills in Guilin and the charm of the West Lake in Hangzhou".

肇庆星湖
Xinghu Lake in Zhaoqing

"Splendid China"
Situated by Shenzhen Bay in the western suburbs of Shenzhen City, Splendid China is a comprehensive miniature scenic area,covering 30 hectares of land. In the scenic area, there are more than 70 spots containing about one hundred famous scenic wonders arranged according to their real locations,including the Great Wall,Terracotta Army of Qin Shihuang's mausoleum which are among the world's eight wonders,etc.

Situated in southern border area and facing Hainan Province across
sea,the Guangxi Zhuang Autonomous Region is bounded by Guangdong,Hu
nan, Guizhou and Yunnan Provinces. Area: over 230000 km².

Guangxi has a mountainous terrain and its northwestern part is high
than the southeastern part, with widely spread limestone.

Because the Tropic of Cancer lies across the middle of the region,it e
joys a subtropic humid monsoon climate, with abundant rainfall and sunsh
The annual mean temperature is 17-23°C and the coastal areas are frost-f
all the year round.

Because of its karst topography, Guangxi possesses a unique enchanting scenery, especia

Scale 1:3550000
0   35.5   71.0   106.5 km

...lin has long enjoyed the reputation of having the most beautiful scenery ...er heaven, and is a famous historical and cultural city and a key tourist ...a in China. The major famous scenic areas include Lijiang River, Xishan ...l and Huashan Hill in Guiping.Besides,Huaping(Flower Ground) in Long-...ng, Xiangbi(Trunk) Hill, Ludi Crag, Diecai Hill, Duxiu Peak,Fubo Hill, ...eya (Crescent) Hill, seaside areas and Liuhou Shrine, etc. ,are all famous scenic spots.

Specialities: the output of anise, cinnamon bark and mangosteen rank the first in China. Pi-...pple in Nanning, Shatian pomelo in Rongxian, etc, are also famous. The well-known handic-...t articles include brocade in Jingxi and Binyang, shell carving in Beihai, stone carving and ink ...ne in Liuzhou, etc.

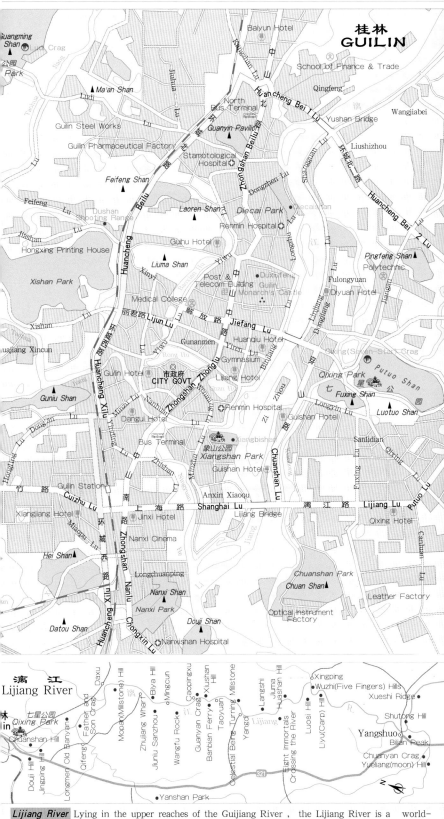

桂林
GUILIN

漓　江
Lijiang River

Lijiang River Lying in the upper reaches of the Guijiang River , the Lijiang River is a world-
famous scenic area . Its 88 km long section from Guilin to Yangshuo is unusually charming , forming
n important part of the Guilin scenery .

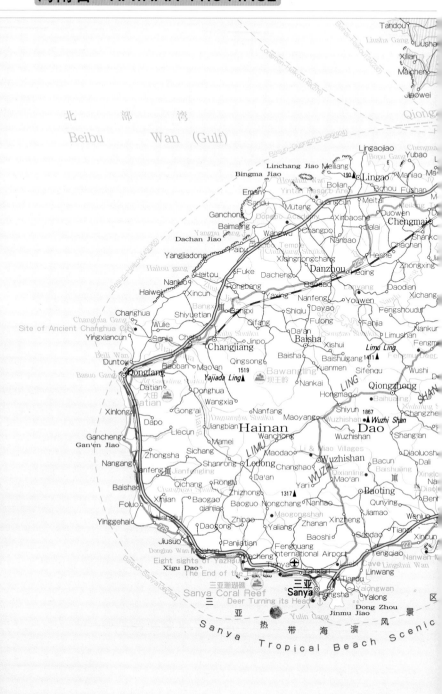

北　部　湾
Beibu　　Wan (Gulf)

Hainan Island is the second largest island in China, which is situated the Nanhai Sea (South China Sea) and facing Guangdong Province acr Qiongzhou Strait. Hainan Province, established in 1988, consists of Hain Island, Xisha Islands,Zhongsha Islands, Nansha Islands and the vast sea are around them. Area: about 340000 km².

The interior of the Hainan island is mountainous, rising to over 1 metres.Tablelands,terraces and plains,with an elevation of less than 100 metr above sea level,occupy about 60% of its total area.

The province has a tropic monsoon climate. It is hot and rainy. There is no frost and sn all the year ruond. The annual mean temperature is up to 22-27° C, and the annual precipitat

00-2600 mm.

Hainan Province possesses a favourable natural environment and is famous
ts bright and beautiful sunshine, vast blue sea, enchanting beaches and
 air.Sanya Tropical Beach Area is one of the national major famous scenic
s.The main historic sites and scenic spots include Wugong Shrine buillt in

Ming Dynasty, Hairui Tomb, Dongpo Academy, Luhuitou(Deer Turning its Head), Dadonghai
at East Sea)Bathing Beach,Tianyahaijiao(the End of the Earth),Underwater Village and Under-
r Forest, etc.

The province is the main tropical crop production base of China and is abundant in rubber,
a, coconut, tropical fruits. The handicraft articles,such as coconut carving,etc, are all famous.

97

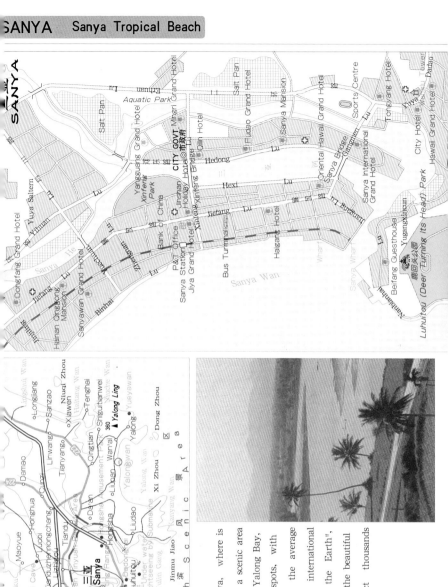

三亚热带海滨
SANYA TROPICAL BEACH

Sanya Tropical Beach Situated in the coastal area of Sanya, where is a beautiful port city of Hainan Province Sanya Tropical Beach is a scenic area renowned both at home and abroad,totaing 212 km². It consists of Yalong Bay, Haitang Bay, "the End of the Earth", Luobi Cave and other scenic spots, with a coastline stretching nearly 100 km frcm east to west. Because the average temperature of the coldest month is 21℃ it has thus become an international tourist resort.The well-known scenic spo·s include "The End of the Earth", "Deer Turning Its Head", Dadonghai ard Yalong Bay, where the beautiful sand beach, green coconut trees, blue sea and fresh air attract thousands of visitors.

99

重庆市 CHONGQING MUNICIPALITY

Standing at the junction of the Changjiang River and Jialing River in the southeastern part of Sichuan Basin, Chongqing is the newly established municipality directly under the Central Government, and the largest industrial city in Southwest China. It is also the hub of communications and famous tourist destination of that area. The city borders on Hubei, Hunan, Guizhou, Sichuan and Shaanxi Provinces. Area: about 82400 km^2.

Chongqing has an uneven terrain consisting of mountainous areas, hilly lands and basins, with the Changjiang River flowing through it from west to east.

It enjoys a subtropic humid monsoon climate. Affected by its particular terrain, the temperature

re is higher than that of the areas in the middle and lower reaches of Changjiang River. The annual mean temperature is 13 – 18 ℃, but the est temperature can reach 43.8 ℃.

Richly endowed by nature, it possesses a great number of famous scen- ots and historic sites. Three Gorges of the Changjiang River, Mt. Jinyun, Simian are the national major famous scenic areas. Moreover, Baiheliang Stone Fish Inscriptions uling, "The Capital of Hell", Dazu Stone Inscriptions, Taibai Crag in Wanzhou, the Lesser Three es of the Daning River, etc, are all well-known scenic sites.

Hot pickled mustard greens, pomelo in Liangping and bamboo woven articles in Dazu, etc, are amous specialities in Chongqing.

重庆
CHONGQING

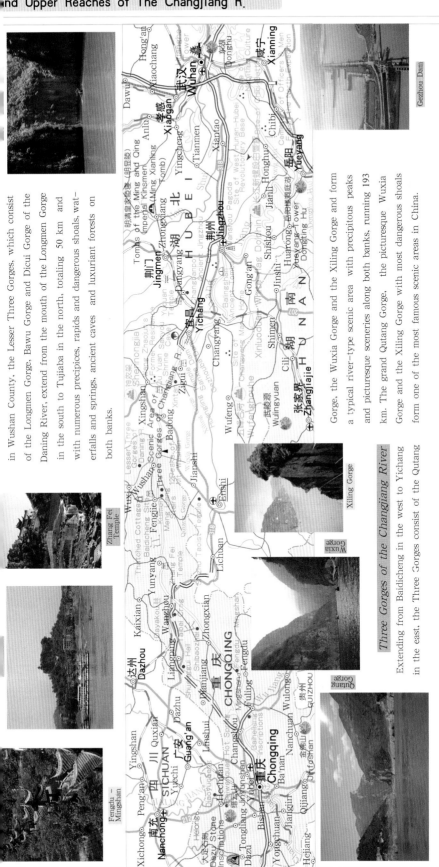

in Wushan County, the Lesser Three Gorges, which consist of the Longmen Gorge, Bawu Gorge and Dicui Gorge of the Daning River, extend from the mouth of the Longmen Gorge in the south to Tujiaba in the north, totaling 50 km and with numerous precipices, rapids and dangerous shoals, waterfalls and springs, ancient caves and luxuriant forests on both banks.

Three Gorges of the Changjiang River

Extending from Baidicheng in the west to Yichang in the east, the Three Gorges consist of the Qutang Gorge, the Wuxia Gorge and the Xiling Gorge and form a typical river-type scenic area with precipitous peaks and picturesque sceneries along both banks, running 193 km. The grand Qutang Gorge, the picturesque Wuxia Gorge and the Xiling Gorge with most dangerous shoals form one of the most famous scenic areas in China.

Gezhou Dam

Zhang Fei Temple

Xiling Gorge

Wuxia Gorge

Qutang Gorge

Fengdu – Mingshan

Located in the upper reaches of the Changjiang (Yangtze) River in the southwest part of China, it is bounded by Shaanxi, Gansu, Qinghai, Yunnan, Guizhou, Xizang(Tibet) and Chongqing Municipality, and has long been known as "a land of plenty" or "Heaven on Earth" for its abundance of produc. Area: about 480000 km².

Sichuan has a varied topography. Mountainous areas occupy its west, a Sichuan Basin and its peripheral highlands predominate in the east. The rel of the eastern region is in sharp contrast to that of the west.

The eastern basin enjoys a subtropic climate, warm and humid, with annual average temperature of 16~18 °C, but the mountainous areas in the west has a highla continental climate, with the annual average temperature of 6~12 °C. The precipitation is lower the west than in the east.

Sichuan has a long history and was once the place of the Ba and Shu ...es during the Spring and Autumn period and the Warring States period, ...erefore,possessing a great number of cultural relics and historic sites.Besi- ... it also boasts many famous mountains and waters,which form a beauti- ...and magnificent natural landscape. There are national major famous ...ic areas, such as Mt. Emei, Mt. Qingcheng-Dujiangyan, Huanglong ...mple-Jiuzhaigou, Ancient Plank Road in Jianmen, Mt. Gongga, Xiling Snowcapped mountain ...the bamboo sea in south Sichuan, etc. Moreover, the scenic areas of Huanglong Temple- ...haigou, and Mt. Emei-Giant Buddha of Leshan have been included in the World Heritages. ...er scenic spots such as Du Fu's Thatched Cottage, etc, are also attractive sites.

...Embroidery in Chengdu, bamboo woven articles, pottery and porcelain, tea, traditional Chinese ...dicine and famous wines are all well-received.

Wuhou Shrine Located in the southern suburbs of Chengdu City was first built in the Western Jin Dynasty to commemorate Zhuge Lia the prime minister of the Shu Han Kingdom in the Three Kingdoms pe The shrine houses 47 statues of historical figures during the Three Ki doms period, and more than 40 upright stone tablets.

Wenshu(Manjusri) Temple Located in Wenshu Street of Cheng City, the temple covers an area of 82 mu of the land, with more than rooms or halls and other houses. In the temple, there are over 100 bro Buddha statues, big or small, cast by famous craftsmen of the Qing Dyna With a careful overall arrangement, the temple looks simple and magnific

106

Du Fu's Thatched Cottage Situated in the southern suburbs of Chengdu, it is the former residence of Du Fu, a great realistic poet of the Tang Dynasty.The main buildings include Shishi Hall,Gongbu Shrine,Tablet pavilion, forming a classical garden. It covers 20 hectares and is one of the famous spots with quiet environment and beautiful scenery.

Mt. Siguniang Situated in Xiaojin County, it is precipitous and magnificent, with its peaks covered with snow all the year round. The dense primeval forests, alpine lakes, glaciers and falls will keep their virginal scenes.

峨眉山
Mt. Emei

Mt. Emei Situated in Eme
an City, Sichuan province, Mt.
mei is a national major famous s
area, and one of the   four fam
Buddhist mountains, covering ab
200 km². It offers the tourists f
spectacular views: the sunrise,
of clouds, Buddha's Light and
sunset glow.

Mt.Emei possesses a great nu
ber of temples, which began to
built in the Western Han Dyna
From the northeastern foot to
summit stand many famous tem
and other buildings, such as Ba
Temple, Fuhu Temple,   Hua
Temple, Chunyang Hall,Shengsh
Pavilion, Wannian Temple,Xixia
(Elephant Bathing) Pool,Jiulao(N
Old Men) Cave,   Xianfeng Tem
and Jinding Top,etc,housing co
tless cultural relics. The bronze
tue of Samantabhadra towering
Wannian Temple is 7.3 metres h
62 tons in weight and is one of
major cultural relics of China.W
its abundant historic sites and fa
nating natural scenery,Mt. Emei
highly valuable in history st
aesthetics, scientific research a
tourism.

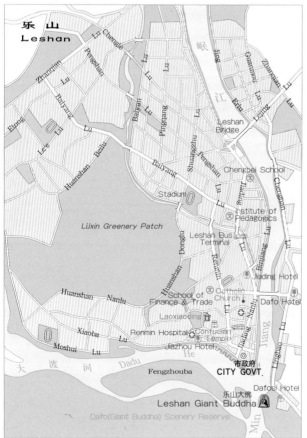

乐山
Leshan

Leshan Giant Buddh
Sitting on the east bank of
Minjiang River and the conf
ence of the Minjiang Riv
Qingyi River and Dadu Riv
east of Leshan City, the Gi
Buddha was hewn on the pr
cipice of Xiluan Peak of M
Lingyun, facing the three to
rential rivers.The project beg
in 713 and ended in 803, spar
ing 90 years. The Giant Budc
is 70 m high and   24 m wi
graceful and poised, ranking
first of the six great sto
buddha statues in China. T
Giant Buddha of Leshan h
been included in the wor
Heritages by UN.

黄 龙
Huanglong

Xuebao Top

Shita Coloured Pool

Yingyue Coloured Pool

Yucui Coloured Pool   Huanglong Temple

Zhongsi Temple

Potang Landscape Pool

Shiting Falls

Guesthouse

Huanglong Scenic Area   Situated in Songpan County of the Aba Zang(Tibet) and Qiang Autonomous Prefecture, Huanglong Scenic   Area covers an area of 700 km², with its main scenic spots being scattered in a 8 km long Valley—Huanglong(Yellow Dragon) valley.   Because of its karst features,   many small colourful lakes like terraced fields can be found on the undulating hillsides and along the valley, while the lakesides   are covered with a layer of sedimentary travertine carbonate, presenting a wonderful sight.

There originally existed three temples —the Front Temple, the Central Temple and the Rear   Temple,   jointly named Huanglong Temple, which were built in the Ming Dynasty. The extant temples are parts of the Central Temple and the Rear Temple. At the upper end of the valley, stands Xuebao Top—a peak perennially covered with snow.

From the bottom of the valley to the mountain top, there exist in sequence subtropical evergreen trees mingled with deciduous broadleaf trees,   coniferous and broadleaf mixed forests, in which   some rare animals,   like Giant Panda,   Golden Monkey are sauntering. With its karst landform, rare flora and fauna resource, and the majestic, precipitous, grotesque and primeval sceneries, Huanglong Scenic Area has won the reputation of "the marvellous scenery in the world".

Jiuzhaigou Scenic Area Located [in N]anping County of the Aba Zang [(Tib]et) and Qiang Autonomous pre[fectu]re, it covers 720 km² of land, [which] possesses lakes, waterfalls, shoals, [stre]ams, snow-capped mountains, fo[rest]s and Tibetan villages. Jiuzhaigou [is] a beautiful and miraculous natural [scen]ery. Most of the scenic spots are [scat]tered in a Y-shaped valley. There [are] more than 100 lakes in the valley. [At t]he upper end of the valley lies a [lak]e called "Changhaizi" (Long Sea), [7 k]m in length and several hundreds [me]tres in width. Its blue waters and [the] inverted reflection of the moun[tain]s, the sky and clouds, attract all [the] visitors. The waterfalls in Jiuzhai[gou], with varied shapes, are seldom [seen] elsewhere. They are scattered [bet]ween the beautiful lakes, of [wh]ich,Nuorilang waterfall is the most [ma]gnificent. Xugjai waterfall, rushing [dow]n from the thicket on the top of [the] steep cliff, is 140 metres wide and [one] of the widest falls in China. [ ] Autumn is the best season to visit [Jiuz]haigou.

九 寨 沟
Jiuzhaigou

Primeval Forest

Multi-coloured Pool
Previous Season Lake

Swan Lake

Rizhai

Next Season Lake

Nuorilang Hotel

High Falls

Zechawazhai   Nuorilang Falls

Xujai Falls

Reeds Lake

Changbanzhai

Baojing Crest

Heliport

Yanadong Hostel

Panxinzhai

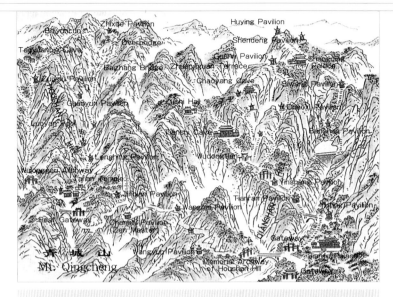

Mt. Qingcheng   Situated 15 km southwest of Dujiangyan City, Mt. Qingcheng, also known as Mt. Chicheng, is one of the famous Taoist mountains in China, with 36 peaks, 72 caves and 108 scenic spots. Its highest peak is 1600 metres above sea level. The extant historic sites here include Tianshidong Temple, Shangqing Palace, Zushi Hall, etc.

Jianfu Palace, situated at the foot of Mt. Qingcheng, is the starting site of the tourist route. Tianshidong, the grandest temple in the mountain, was first built in the Sui Dynasty. The extant structure was built in the Qing Dynasty. Shangqing Palace, standing on the highest peak, was first built in the Jin Dynasty, with a magnificent and symmetric layout.

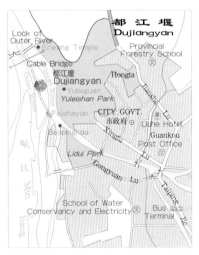

Dujiangyan Irrigation System   Situated i Dujiangyan City in the upper reaches of the Minjian River, Dujiangyan Irrigation System is a world-famou ancient large irrigation project. According to legend, was built by the people led by the local official Li Bi and his son of the Qin State, the Warring States perio After the irrigation project was completed,Minjiang Riv Was controlled to irrigate the vast plain in west Sichua

This area also possesses beautiful scenery of gree hills and clear waters and historic sites. Lidui Park Erwang Temple, Yuleishan Park and Dujiangyan Irrig ation System itself are famous tourist sites.

South Sichuan's Bamboo Sea   Situated in Changning and Jiang'an Counties, the Sea of Bamboos seldom seen in the country covers an area of about 120 km^2, spreading over more than 20 ridges and hills and was classified as one of the major national scenic areas in 1988. This area possesses a unique scenery and numerous scenic spots, among which, Tianbaozhai, Tianhuang Temple, Qinglong(Green Dragon) Lake, Guanyun Pavilion, the Site of Ancient Battlefield, Chahua (Camellia) Hill, Colourful Falls, Feicui(Jadeite) Corridor and the Thirteen Bridges over Huaxi Brook are praised as the " Ten Extre-mely Beautiful Sights" of the Sea of Bamboos.

西岭雪山
Xiling Snowberg

Xiling Snowberg Standing in Dayi County about 100 km away from Chengdu City, Xiling Snowberg occupies an area of over 480 km², with natural alpine sceneries as its distinguishing features. It has snow-capped mountains, vast primeval forests, numerous rare plants and animals, and perennial torrents and falls. The magnificent Mt. Miaoling is covered with snow all the year round and towers to the sky, which can be seen from Chengdu City during sunny days. Xiling Snowberg can be divided into five scenic areas with varied beautiful sceneries. The Scenic Area of Grotesque Peaks and Rocks contains Grotesque Stone Forest, Wuding Hill and Taixu Valley, etc; Huashiyu Scenic Area is like a 3.7 km long landscape painting gallery, where the main scenic spots are Yuquan Spring (Fish Spring), Zhenzhu (Pearl) Spring, Feiquan Cave and the Nine Falls and a Thread of Sky; Qianshui Rafting Scenic Area is famous for its waterfalls, such as Colourful Falls, Fengwei Falls and Feilian Cave; and the Scenic Area of Sweet-scented Osmanthus and Azalea has such scenic spots as Guanyun Terrace, Yuangu Valley, Dashanmen Gate, Baishagang, Hongshijian and Riyueping, etc.

Mt. Gongga Standing 55 km south of 〔Lu〕ding County, Mt. Gongga is 7556m above 〔sea〕 level, the highest peak in Sichuan Province, 〔cover〕ing an area of about 20000 km². Around 〔the〕 main peak, there stand over 100 ice-〔cove〕red peaks of 5000-6000 m above sea 〔level〕,forming a magnificent sight.Mt. Gongga 〔is a〕 sacred mountain to the Tibetan ethnic 〔grou〕p, which possesses glaciers, alpine lakes, 〔hot〕 springs, rare animals and plants, and 〔num〕erous temples, buildings with ethnic style, 〔mak〕ing a large natural scenic area of 10000

Jianmen Shu Path The ancient Shu 〔Path〕, a plank roadway of over 150 km 〔buil〕t in ancient times, was once the tho-〔roug〕hfare from Hanzhong and Ningqiang 〔of Sha〕anxi Province to Guangyuan, Jian'ge and 〔Miany〕ng of Sichuan Province.Along the path, 〔ther〕e exist extraodinary natural sceneries 〔and〕 many historic sites.such as the remains 〔of th〕e plank roadway at Chaotian Taoist 〔Tem〕ple,the site of Ancient Battlefield of the 〔Thre〕e Kingdom Period, etc.

贡嘎山
Mt. Gongga

Mt. Gongga

Icefalls

Tower-like Rock

Glacial Arch

Viewing Stage

Glacial Stone Mushroom

No. 3 Campsite

Glacial Gateway

Helu Pavilion

No. 2 Campsite

No. 1 Campsite

Shashuping

Moxi

111

贵州省 GUIZHOU PROVINCE

Situated in the eastern part of the Yunnan–Guizhou Plateau in southwe China, Guizhou borders on Sichuan, Yunnan, Hunan provinces, Guangxi Zhuan Autonomous Region and Chongqing Minicipality. Area: over 170000 km².

Guizhou Province is a part of the Yun–Gui Plateau. The entire terr slopes at a steep angle from the centre toward the north, east and south, wi an average elevation of over 1000 metres. In the limestone areas, the land surf ce is incised strongly, namely so called karst characterized by precipitous s pes, protuberant mountains, caverns and subterranean streams, and steep go

It enjoys a subtropic highland humid monsoon climate, with warm summer and mild win The annual average temperature is 10–20 ℃. Rainfall is plentiful, with an annual mean precipita of 900–1500 mm.

Guizhou is one of the regions with developed tourist industry in China.
national major famous scenic areas include the well-known Huangguo-
Waterfall, Wuyang River, Hongfeng Lake, Zhijin Cave, Longgong (Dragon
e) Cave, Zhangjiang River, etc. Others are Mt. Qianling, Jiaxiu Tower,
the Site of Zunyi Meeting, etc.

Guizhou has a large number of minority people, therefore, the local
itions and customs of various minority nationalities are of graceful bearings.

The province boasts plenty of famous local products. The world-famous Maotai Wine is made
Wax printing in Anshun, Pottery in Pintang, Lacquerware in Bijie and Meijiang tea and Mao-
tea are all well received by the tourists.

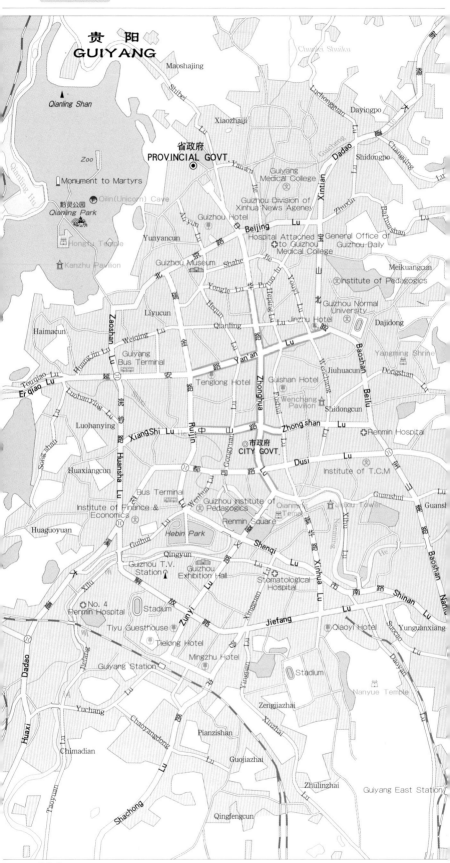

贵阳
GUIYANG

Maoshajing

Qianling Shan

Shibei Lu

Xiaozhaiji

Guizheng Dadao

Luchonggguan

Dayingpo

Shidongpo

Changqing Lu

Xintian

Zoo

省政府
PROVINCIAL GOVT.

Yanin

Guiyang
Medical College

Monument to Martyrs

Qilin (Unicorn) Cave

Guizhou Division of
Xinhua News Ageney

Zhuxin

Baihuashan Lu

黔灵公园
Qianling Park

Guizhou Hotel

Hospital Attached
to Guizhou
Medical College

Beijing Lu

General Office of
Guizhou Daily

Hongfu Temple

Yunyancun

Guizhou Museum

Shahe

Hequn

Puruo lu

Youyi

Institute of Pedagogics

Meikuangcun

Kanzhu Pavilion

北

Yongle lu

北

Guizhou Normal
University

Dajidong

Liyucun

Qianling

Jinzhu Hotel

Haimacun

Weiqing Lu

Yan an Lu

Baoshan Beilu

Yangming Shrine

Touqiao Lu

Huangjin Lu

Guiyang
Bus Terminal

Jiuhuacun

Dongshan

Er qiao Lu

Luohanjing Lu

Tenglong Hotel

Zhonghua

Guishan Hotel

Fushui

Wenchang
Pavilion

Shidongcun

Luohanying

XiangShi Lu

Ruijin

Zhong shan Lu

Renmin Hospital

Huaxiangcun

Huansha Lu

市政府
CITY GOVT.

Dusi Lu

Institute of T.C.M

Guanshui

Huaguoyuan

Institute of Finance &
Economics

Bus Terminal

Wenhua Lu

Guizhou Institute of
Pedagogics

Renmin Square

Qianmi
Temple

Jiaxiu Tower

Guansl

Hebin Park

Guihui

Qingyun

Shenqi Lu

Xinhua Lu

Namming

Xihu

Baoshan Nanlu

Guizhou T.V.
Station

Guizhou
Exhibition Hall

Stomatological
Hospital

Shinan Lu

No. 4
Renmin Hospital

Stadium

Zun yi lu

Jiefang

Qiaoyi Hotel

Yunguanxiang

Tiyu Guesthouse

Tielong Hotel

Xihu

Jiefang

Mingzhu Hotel

Guiyang Station

Yingshan

Stadium

Dadao

Nanyue Temple

Yuchang

Chaoyangdong

Pianzishan

Xinzhai

Zengjiazhai

Huaxi

Chimadian

Guojiazhai

Zhulinzhai

Guiyang East Station

Taoyuan

Shachong

Qingfengcun

Huangguoshu　Located in the Zhenning Bouyei and Miao Autonomous County and 45 km southwest of Anshun, the scenic area possesses more than 20 waterfalls and cascades including Huangguoshu Waterfall, Doupotang Waterfall, Guanling Waterfall, etc, but Huangguoshu Waterfall is the most magnificent. When the river swells in summer, the waterfall is over 80 metres wide and 74 metres high, with waters roaring down at a rate of 2000 cubic metres per second into Xiniu (Rhinoceros) pool.

Doupotang Waterfall, located on the upper reaches of the river, 21 metres high and 105 metres wide, is the widest one among the falls in that area.

Huangguoshu Scenic Area has also beautiful natural scenery with clusters of peaks and wonderful caves. The most wonderful caves are Longgong(Dragon Palace) Cave, Tianxing Cave and Xiniu (Rhinoceros) Cave, etc. Besides, the Bouyei and Miao minority people living in this area are not only hospitable but good at singing and dancing, and their local folk customs attract all the visitors.

Longgong Scenic Area　Situated 27 km south of Anshun City, it is a scenic area consisting of Longgong Falls, Tianchi Lake, underground rivers and stone forest, etc. Longgong Cave is a 400 metres long underground river linking several pools with openings above. Now, only the first one fifth of them is open to the public, which is 800 metres long and divided into six natural "halls". When boating in the cave, visitors could view a wonderful sight.

Hongfeng Lake　Situated 40 km west of Guiyang City, it is a reservoir built on the Maotiao River and the largest one in the Guizhou Plateau, which has the fame of "the pearl on the plateau". It has a water surface of 57 km². Because of its zigzag coast line and complicated branching streams, the lake is divided into four parts with varied sceneries. In the lake, there stand numerous islets, on some of which, many beautiful buildings of the Dong style have been set up, such as bridges, drum tower and the Dong villages.

云南省 YUNNAN PROVINCE

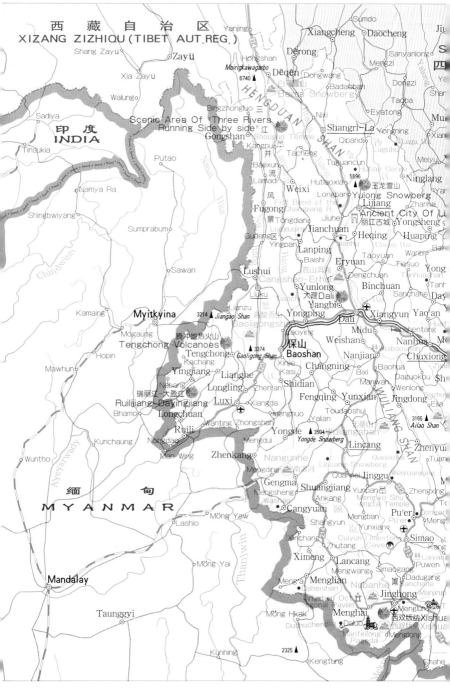

Located in the southwestern frontier of China and the southwestern pa
Of the Yunnan-Guizhou Plateau, Yunnan Province is bounded by Guangx
Guizhou, Sichuan and Xizang (Tibet) Auto. Reg., and adjoins Myanmar, La
and Vietnam on the west and south. Area: over 380000 km².

Yunnan is a mountain and plateau region, and mountainous areas an
plateau make up 94% of its total area.

It enjoys a tropic highland humid monsoon climate, characterized by co
summer and warm winter. It is like spring all the year round. The annua
average temperature is 13-20°C and the annual rainfall is 1100 mm.

Yunnan possesses lofty mountains, deep valleys and torrential rivers, and is inhabited b

1:5450000

Scale 0 54.5 109.0 163.5 km

...e than 20 nationalities with different customs, which form the principal
...res of its sceneries and tourist industry. The national major famous scenic
...s include Dianchi Lake in Kunming, Lunan Stone forest, Dali, Xishuang-
...na, Yulong Snowberg in Lijiang, Tengchong Volcanoes, Jiuxiang, Jianshui,
...ng R.–Daying R., and the scenic area of the Three Rivers Running Side
...Side, etc. The ancient City of Lijiang has been listed in the World Heritages. Besides, the tou-
...activities with distinctive ethnic features attract all the tourists both from home and abroad.

    The province boasts abundant famous local product. Yunnan cigarette, Yunnan medicine,   and
...nan tea such as Dianlu, Pu'er, Dianhong, and Yunnan Ham, etc., are all famous specialities.

Daguan Tower is situated in Daguan Park, 2km southwest of Kunming City.

Dianchi Lake Situated about 2km southwest of Kunmi Dianchi Lake is a highland limestone fault lake, and one of major scenic areas in China, covering an area of about 300km The elevation of its water surface is over 1800 metres above level and the average water depth is 5.5 metres. There are ov 20 rivers emptying into the lake . The vast misty Dianchi La enjoys the fame of " A Pearl on the Yunnan−Guizhou Plateau Around the lake , there exist a great number of famous moun tains and scenic sites.

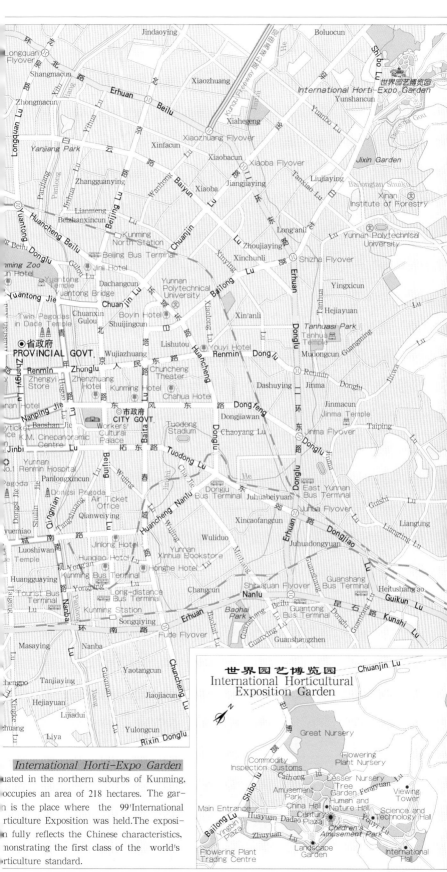

International Horti-Expo Garden

uated in the northern suburbs of Kunming,
occupies an area of 218 hectares. The gar-
n is the place where the 99'International
rticulture Exposition was held.The exposi-
n fully reflects the Chinese characteristics,
monstrating the first class of the world's
rticulture standard.

世界园艺博览园
International Horticultural Exposition Garden

Stone Forest　Cangshan–Erhai　Xishuangbanna

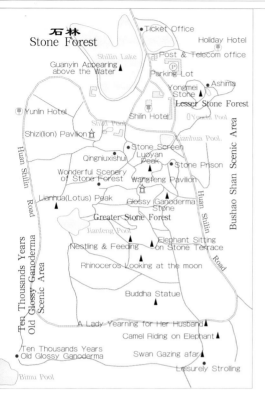

Stone Forest Situated in the northeastern part of the Shilin Yi Autonomous County, Stone Forest is one of the major famous scenic areas in China,covering an area of 350km². The most wonderful sites include the Greater Stone Forest, the lesser Stone Forest, the Outer Stone Forest and underground Stone Forest, ect. It enjoys a great prestige both at home and abroad.

Cangshan–Erhai　Erhai Lake famous alpine freshwater lake with an of 246km², is situated to the north of City. The vast expanse of misty, roll green waters make Erhai Lake a wond ful scenic area. Furthermore, there a great number of scenic spots and hist sites in the area, such as "Three Pagod in Chongsheng Temple,etc.

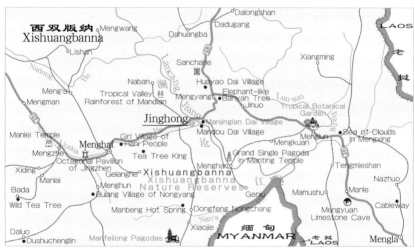

Xishuangbanna This famous scenic area usually refers to the Xishuangbanna Dai Autonomous Prefecture in the southwestern part of Yunnan Province, with a total area of 19184 km². Because of the rolling mountain ridges in this area and being affected by the monsoon, it is hot and rainy here. There are vast tropical rainforests, exotic flowers and rare grasses. In the virgin forests, Golden monkeys, elephants,rhinoceroses and peacocks are found.Xishuangbanna has been known as "An Emerald in the Plant Kingdom" , "The Animal Kingdom" and " The Home of Peacocks", especially the tropical rainforest in Menglun Valley. The historic sites are the White Pagodas in Manfeilong, the Octagonal Pavilion of Jingzhen, ect.

拉萨
LHASA

Potala Palace is Situated in Lhasa City

Lying in the southwestern part of Qinghai–Xizang Plateau, known a "the Roof of the World", Xizang borders on India, Nepal, Sikhim, Bhuta Myanmar and adjoins Sichuan, Qinghai, Yunnan and Xinjiang Uygur Auto- nomous Region. Area: over 1200000 km².

Xizang is the principal part of Qinghai–Xizang Plateau, surrounded b mountain masses, including Qomolangma Peak with the world's maximu elevation of 8848 metres above sea level. There are numerous alpine lake torrential rivers and magnificent Buddhist temples, and therefore, it has lon been an ideal region for mountain-climbing, scientific investigation, exploration, tourism and Buddhist activities.

122

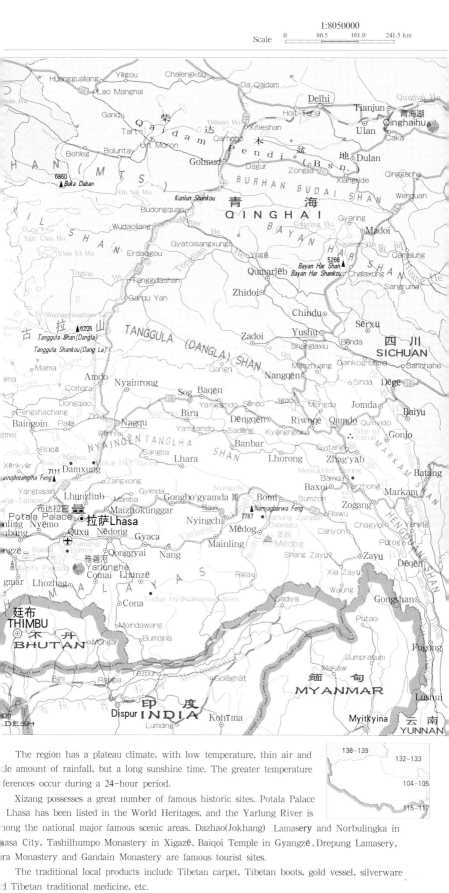

The region has a plateau climate, with low temperature, thin air and
[litt]le amount of rainfall, but a long sunshine time. The greater temperature
[dif]ferences occur during a 24-hour period.

Xizang possesses a great number of famous historic sites. Potala Palace
[in] Lhasa has been listed in the World Heritages, and the Yarlung River is
[am]ong the national major famous scenic areas. Dazhao(Jokhang) Lamasery and Norbulingka in
[Lh]asa City, Tashilhumpo Monastery in Xigazê, Baiqoi Temple in Gyangzê, Drepung Lamasery,
[Se]ra Monastery and Gandain Monastery are famous tourist sites.

The traditional local products include Tibetan carpet, Tibetan boots, gold vessel, silverware
[an]d Tibetan traditional medicine, etc.

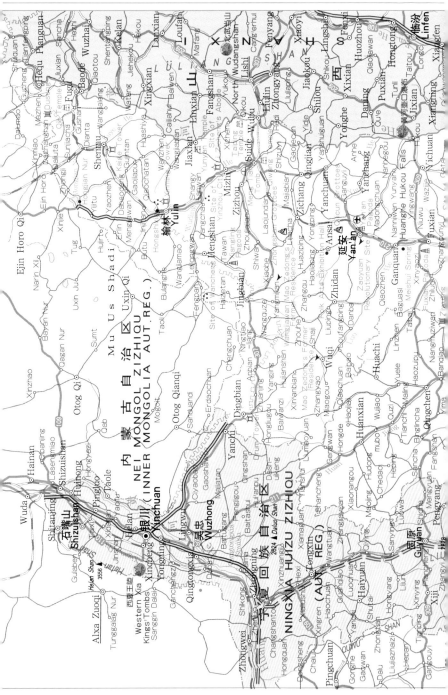

Situated in the middle reaches of the Huanghe River, the province borders on Nei Mongol Autonomous Region, Ningxia Hui Autonomous Region, Gasu, Sichuan, Hubei, Shanxi and Shandong Provinces, and Chongqing Municipality. Area: over 190000 km².

The Province comprises three distinct geographic natural regions — the northern upland plateau, the southern mountainous region and the Guanzhor (Central Shaanxi) Plain.

Shaanxi Province is located in a subtropic humid monsoon climate zor Its northern part has a dry winter and spring, but a rainy summer and autumn, while its southe part enjoys a temperate humid climate, with abundant rainfall.

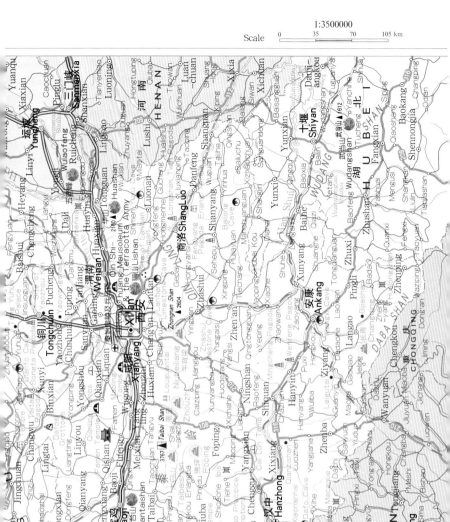

With abundant historic sites and cultural relics, and famous mountains
rivers, Shannxi has a developed tourist industry. The national major
us scenic areas, such as Mt.Huashan, Mt.Lishan in Lintong, Mt.Tiantai
aoji, are all well-known to visitors both from home and abroad. The
d-famous Qin Shihuang Mausoleum was included in the World Heritag-
1987. Other famous scenic spots include Dayan (Wild Goose) Pagoda,
Forest in Xi'an, Hot Spring in Lintong, Banpo Primitive Society Ruins and Mt. Cuihua, etc.
Local products, such as pomegranate in Lintong, red date in Qingjian, Maojian tea in Ziyang
ll very famous, and the Tang Tricoloured glazed Pottery is also well-received by visitors.

西安
XI'AN

The History Museum is situated in the south of Xi'an.

Dayan Pagoda is standing in The south of Xi'an.

华山 Mt.Huashan

Mt.Huashan Standing in Huayin County, 120 km east of Xi'an City, the mountain is noted for its sheer cliffs and towering peaks. It is one of the five great mountains in China and the sacred mountain to Taoists. It is known as the Western Sacred Mountain. Mt. Huashan has five famous peaks, namely, East Peak, West Peak, South Peak, North Peak and Central Peak, of which South Peak, soaring 2200 metres above sea level, is the highest. The peaks are connected by a series of sharp ridges, generally only wide enough to accommodate one person at a time. Along the touring route, tourists can visit many amazing ancient buildings perched on the knife-sharp edges.

The Vicinity of Xi'an Like a giant history museum, the Central Shaanxi Plain possesses great number of famous scenic spots and historic sites, demonstrating the once most brilliant chapters of China's history. The most famous historic sites include the world-famous Terracotta Army Emperor Qin Shihuang Mausoleum, Emperor Huang Mausoleum, Huaqing Hot Spring at the northern foot of Mt. Lishan, Qianling Tomb and Famen Temple, ect., of which the Terracotta Army is the most famous and is known as "the Eighth Wonder of the World". Discovered in 1974, three vaults have been excavated, in which about 8000 life-size terracotta warriors and 600 horse sculptures, and over 10000 real weapons carried by the warriors were unearthed.

Now, still more excavations are being done, and more cultural relics are expected to be unearthed.

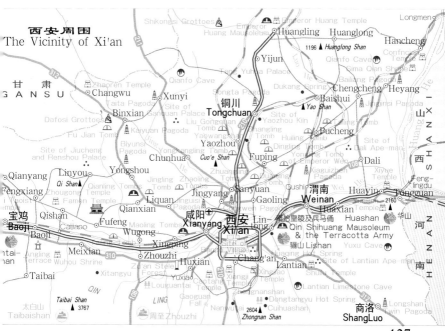

Situated in the upper reaches of the Huanghe River, northwest China, Gansu Province borders on Ningxia, Shaanxi, Nei Mongol, Sichuan, Qinghai, Xinjiang and Mongolia. Area: more than 390000 km².

Gansu Province occupies a long narrow area at the junction of Loess Plateau, Mongolia Plateau and Qinghai-Xizang (Tibet) Plateau. Mountainous area and plateau make up 70% of the total land and the most parts of the province are as high as 1000-3000 metres above sea level.

The province belongs to the temperate monsoon climate zone, and is one of the arid provinces in China. The annual mean temperature is 4-14 ℃ and the annual rainfall is merely 300-560 mm.

Gansu has a developed tourist industry. The world-famous ancient Silk
[Roa]d once passed through the province and left a great number of historic
[site]s. The national major scenic areas include Mt.Maiji,   Mt.Kongdong,
[Ming]sha Hill-Yueya (crescent) Spring, and Jiayuguan Pass, etc. Mogao
[Grot]toes in Dunhuang were listed in the World Heritages in 1987 by UNESCO.
[Othe]r historic sites, such as Binglingsi Grottoes, Yulin Grottoes, Shuiliandong Grottoes, Labrang
[Tem]ple, Haizang Temple etc, are all well-known to tourists.

[B]ailan melon, Chinese angelica, black melon-seeds and lily,etc, are all   famous local products.
[Its] traditional handicraft articles, such as jade carving, are well-received by the vistiors.

129

兰州
LANZHO

Jiayuguan Pass Situated in the Southwest of Jiayuguan City,it is the west terminal point of the Great Wall. The pass was built in the Ming Dynasty and was a hotly contested strategic point in ancient times.The magnificent pass has two gates, two gate towers and four turrets on its four corners, covering 33500 m².

Mt. Kongtong Located 30 km west of Pinglian City, Mt. Kongtong is a branch range of Liupai Mountains. Since the Qin and Han Dynasties, temple and Taoist temples began to be built in succesion,an the mountain became a famous sacred mountain Taoists.Pagoda of the Ming Dynasty,Taihe palace o the Qing Dynasty are the main extant buildings.

Mogao Grottoes

Situated at the eastern foot of Mingsha Hill in Dunhuang, Mogao Grottoes were first hewn in 366 A. D.by eminent Monk Le Zun, and more than 1000 grottoes were hewn.

Mt. Maiji

Situated about 45 km southeast of Tianshui City, Mt. Maiji is famous for its grottoes, one of the national major famous scenic areas in China.

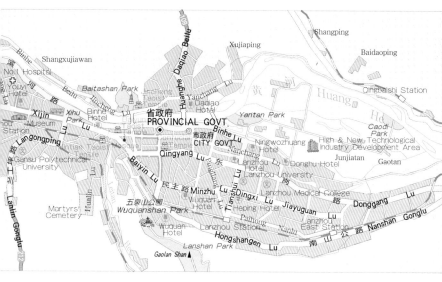

古丝绸之路
The Silk Road

Mingsha Hill-Yueya Spring

Situated about 6 km south of Dunhuang City, Mingsha Hill, also known as Shensha Hill, occupies an area of about 800 km², with a relative height of 250 m and Yueya(Crecent) Spring, lying at its northern foot, is a crescent-like pool, 200 metres long and more than 50 metres wide.

Situated in the northeastern part of the Qinghai-Xizang(Tibet) Plateau Northwest China, Qinghai Province is known as the "Roof of the World" a with Xizang Autonomous Region. It borders on Gansu, Sichuan, Xizang Aut omous Region and Xinjiang Uygur Autonomous Region. Area: 720000 km².

Most of the province consists of mountains and high plateaus, with average elevation of over 3000 metres above sea level. Between the mountains are broad basins, rolling hilly areas and extensive flat tableland.

The province has a typical continental climate, characterized by the c windy and cold weather. The annual mean temperature is −5°– 8°C and the annual precipita is 250–550 mm.

It possesses famous mountains and great rivers. The famous rivers such as the Changjiang(Yangtze) River and the Huanghe River all rise here. The beautiful glaciers and rolling lofty mountains offer the ideal places for mountain-climbing and scientific investigations. Qinghai Lake, the largest inland salt lake in China, is a national major famous scenic area. There stands a Bird Island in the northwestern part of the lake, where over 100000 various birds are dwelling from May to autumn every year, presenting a splendid sight. Other famous historic sites include Tar Monastery in Huangzhong, Grand Mosque in Xining, etc.

The specialities mainly include marmot skin, carpet, lambskin, and handicraft articles such as silver ware, ornaments and Zang-style knives.

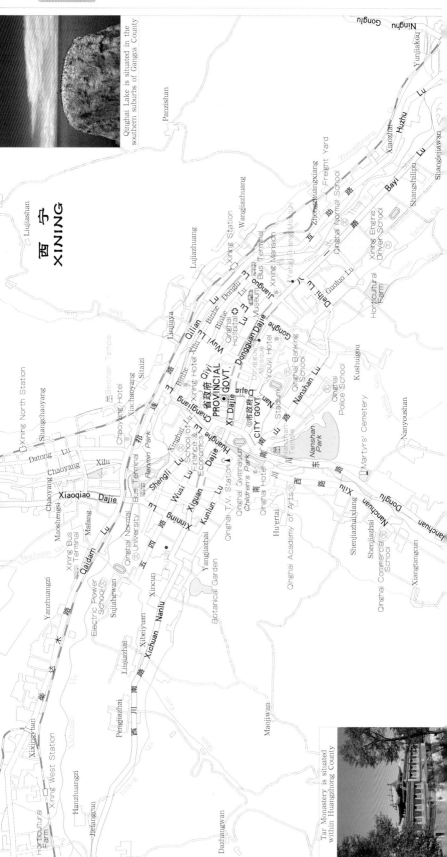

西宁
XINING

Qinghai Lake is situated in the southern suburbs of Gangca County

Tar Monastery is situated within Huangzhong County

Xumishan Grottoes

It is located at the northern end of Liupan Mountains. Now, 20 odd grottoes have been preserved intact.

Western Xia Kings' Tombs

The tombs is situated at the eastern foot of Mt. Helan, some 30 km west of Yinchuan City.

135

Qahar
Jun Bel
Tar Atu
Xilin Gol
甘肃
GANSU
Qagan Hutug
Zhongjiaquan

Lasengmiao
Shitanjing Shizuishan
Maliantan Wuzha Bayan Tohoi
Wudangshan Guleben Ruijigou 石嘴山 Huinong
Shizuishan
Taixi Huangtiangqiao
Helan Shan Conggang Pavilion
Helanshan Cliff Painting 3556 山 Pingluo
Alxa Zuoqi 贺兰山 Taole
Helanshan Excursion Area Yaotu

Tulantai 腾 格 里 沙 漠 Jinshan Chanshan Taoli
Tengger Shamo Toudaodun
西夏王陵 Helan Bulag
Western Xia Kings' Tombs Xincheng
内蒙古自治区 Sanggin Dala 银川 Yinchuan Mo
NEI MONGOL ZIZHIQU Hedong Airport
(INNER MONGOLIA AUT. REG.) Yongning Linhe Otog Qianqi
Obotu Wanghong Site of Shuidonggou Subbing Sanduandi
Yuquanyingzhan Lingwu
吴忠 Huiminxiang Dongtang
Qingtongxia Dadu Wuzhong Gaomiao Gaoshawo
108 Pagodas Qingtongxia 东武白芨滩 Donmaping
Guangwu Qingtongxia Shuiku Baitugang Lingwu Baijitan Yanchi
Qingtongxia Shuiku Shigouyi Mallatan Wanglejing
Zhaobishan Mushou Shan Ya'ergou Yanchi
▲ 1774 Fengligou Haojiatai Qingshan Yanchiqiao
Shikengsi Grottoes Zaoyuan Ma'enzhuang Dingbian
Tengger Els Gaomiao Temple Qingtongxia Huianpu Hongliugou
Xiaohong- shanzhan Zhongwei Baima Gunduan Dashukeng 陕
Changlushuizhan Zhenluo Shikou Shuitao Langbuzhang SHAAN
Nanchangtan Zhongning Weizhou Fengdekeng Wangban
Shapotou Dazhaniang Hongsipu Daluo Shan Kangjic Pagoda Mahuangshan
Wufo Chenshui Changshantou Tupo ▲ 2624 Mengcheng Jiyuan
Jingzhuang Xinzhuangji Tianshui Qintuanzhuang Lubb
Yongxin Xiang Shan ▲ 2356 Taoshan Jijia Shancheng Gengwan
Shuanglong Saoyanjing Hanjiaoshui Xiamaguan Qiaochun
Batan Dongsheng Baiyaozi Dingjiatang Grand Mosque Bailitan Yuance
Wuhe Xingren Xutao Xinglong Tongxin Maliagaozhuang Hongde Huanxian
Pingchuan Jing'an Haozhuan Wangtuan Yuwang Nanliqigou Wu
Shuiquan Luoshan Shuangji Liwang Zhangjiayuan Xiaonangou Mubo
Liuchuan Gonghe Yanchi Saotaisi Yangfang Yanglu Gancheng Liuyuanzi Hedao
Jingyuan Tiandu Shan ▲ 2703 Shutai Balzui Diying Maojing Chedao
Fanjiayao Gaowan Haiyuan Caowa Gaotai Quzi
Silong Zhongtian Guanmenshan Hucheng Sanying Luowa Hedao Tianchi
Caoxian Dalu Liujiazhaizi Guanzhuang Xumishan Grottoes Tanshan Binglincha Sansh
Shanghuacha Guochengyi Hepan Xinyuan Huangduobu Yangchang Chedao
Gongjing Touzhaizi Sifangwu Lijian Shanmacha Shagou Guanting Wangwa Qing
Bailu Hanjiacha Xinying Zhongne Guyuan Caomiao Mengyuan 庆阳
Gancaodian Lujiagou Chaijiamen Baliwang Xiji Xiapu Hechuan Wulingshan Fangshan Qing
Jingjiaquan Xigongyi Tianping 309 Xizhai Piancheng Kaicheng Grottoes Chengyang Mengba
Gaoya Huining Zhaijiasuo Subao Jiangtai Zhangyi Pengyang Honghe Zhenyuan
Xiangquan Xintianpu Pingfeng Dawan ▲ 2928 ▲ Liupan Shan Xincheng Pingdao Xi
Mahe Lijiabu Jieshipu Yudiepu Liancai Haodian Longde Jingyuan 平凉 Pingliang Yudu
Beizhai Tong'anyi Maying Taoshan Wenbu Baimian 岽崆山 Kongtongshan 甘 肃
G A N S U Jingming Gangou Weirong Nanhu Dazhai Huasuo Jinghuan Luohand
Xiangquan Shengou Leida Liupanshan Cedi Chang
Liangyi Chongxin SHA

India inset / regional map:
32-33
124-12
128
129

Situated in the middle reaches of the Huanghe River, Ningxia Hui Autonomous Region is bounded by Shaanxi , Gansu Provinces and Nei Mongol Autonomous Region. Area: over 66000 km².

The region extends across the Loess Plateau and Nei Mongol Plateau, with an average height of over 1000 metres above sea level. Mountainous areas occupy 15.8% of its total land.

Ningxia enjoys a temperate continental climate . The annual mean temperature is 5-10 ℃ and the yearly precipitation is 200-600 mm.

Ningxia possesses a great number of historic sites, among which, the famous Western Xia Kings' Tombs are the most attractive.

The "Five Treasures of Ningxia" are the famous special products in five colours, including the fruit of Chinese wolfberry in red, the licorice root in yellow, the inkstone in blue, the Tan-sheepskin in white and the flagelliform nostoc in black.

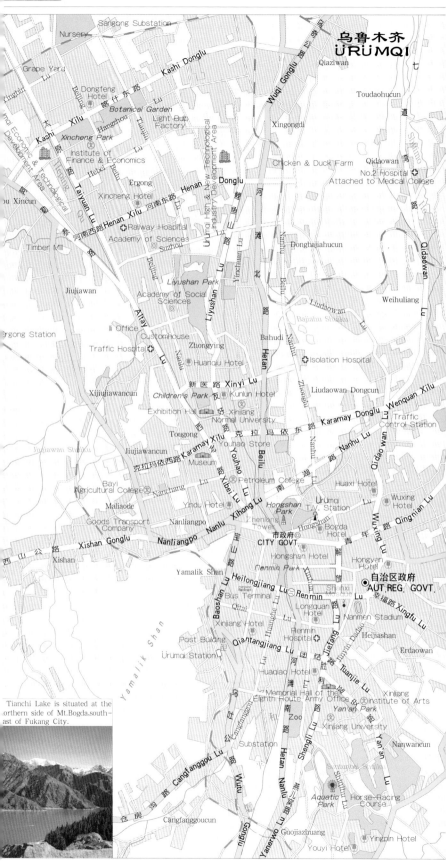

乌鲁木齐
URUMQI

Sangong Substation

Nursery

Qiaziwan

Grape Yard

Toudaohucun

Kashi Donglu

Dongfeng Hotel

喀什东路

Xingongdi

Botanical Garden

Light Bulb Factory

Xincheng Park

Kashi Xilu

Institute of Finance & Economics

Qidaowan

Chicken & Duck Farm

No.2 Hospital
Attached to Medical College

Donglu

Ergong

Xincheng Hotel

河南东路

Henan Xilu

Henan

Railway Hospital
Academy of Sciences

Suzhou

Dongbajiahucun

Timber Mill

Weihuliang

Jiujiawan

Liyushan Park

Liudaowan

Academy of Social Sciences

Bajiahu Shuiku

Ergong Station

Ili Office

Customhouse

Bahudi

Traffic Hospital

Zhongying

Isolation Hospital

Huanqiu Hotel

新医路 Xinyi Lu

Liudaowan Dongcun

Xijiujiawancun

Children's Park

Kunlun Hotel

Exhibition Hall

Xinjiang
Normal University

Wenquan Xilu

Traffic Control Station

Karamay Donglu

Tougong

克拉玛依东路

Jiujiawancun

Karamay Xilu

Youhao Store

克拉玛依西路

Museum

Petroleum College

Huaxi Hotel

Wuxing Hotel

Bayi Agricultural College

Nanchang

Yindu Hotel

Xibei Lu

Hongshan Park

Urumqi T.V. Station

Maliaode

Xihong Lu

Zhenlong Tower

Bogda Hotel

Goods Transport Company

Nanliangpo

Nanlu

Hongshan

市政府
CITY GOVT.

Hongyan Hotel

Xishan Gonglu

Nanliangpo

Hongshan Hotel

自治区政府
AUT.REG. GOVT.

Xishan

Yamalik Shan

Renmin Park

Renmin

Shanxi

Heilongjiang Lu

Bus Terminal

Longquan Hotel

Nanmen Stadium

Qitai

Xinjiang Hotel

Renmin Hospital

Heijiashan

Post Building

Qiantangjiang Lu

Erdaowan

Urumqi Station

Huaqiao Hotel

Memorial Hall of the Eighth Route Army Office

Xinjiang Institute of Arts

Yan'an Park

Zoo

Xinjiang University

Nanwancun

Substation

Cangfanggod Lu

Aquatic Park

Horse-Racing Course

Cangfanggoucun

Guojiazhuang

Yingpin Hotel

Youyi Hotel

Tianchi Lake is situated at the northern side of Mt.Bogda,south-east of Fukang City.

Situated in the northwestern border area of China, Xinjiang Uygur Aut
nomous Region covers nearly 1/6 of the total area of China. It borders on Mo
golia, Russia, Kazakhstan, Kyrgyzstan, Tajikistan, Pakistan and adjoins Gans
Qinghai and Xizang Autonomous Region. In ancient times, Xinjiang was a par
of the West Regions, where the world-famous Silk Road of the Han and Tar
Dynasties passed through.

Xinjiang is encircled by high mountains, with large, lower basins and hig
mountains lying alternately within it. Tarim Basin is the largest inland basin
China, while the Chogori Feng (Qogir Peak) is the highest in this area, with an elevation of 8611
metres above sea level.

It has a typical continental climate, with little amount of rainfall. Greater temperature diff

...nces exist between south and north of Tianshan Mountains.

Xinjiang is a multi-nationality region and possesses lofty snow-capped ...untains, vast deserts, large basins and many famous historic sites. Tianchi ...ke on Tianshan Mountain is a national major famous scenic area. Other ...nic spots, such as Qianfo Grottoes, Idkah Mosque, Grape Valley in Turp-..., and many remains of ancient cities or castles, Xinjiang minority nation-...ties' Folk Custom Exhibition Hall, are all well-known to the visiotrs, while the vast pasture ...nds in Hongshan Mountain and Nanshan Mountain present a fascinating grassland scenery.

The specialities in Xinjiang Uygur Autonomous Region are famous in China. Hami melons, ...megranate in Yecheng, walnut in Aksu, Lambskin in Kuqa and many others, are all famous ...roughout the country.

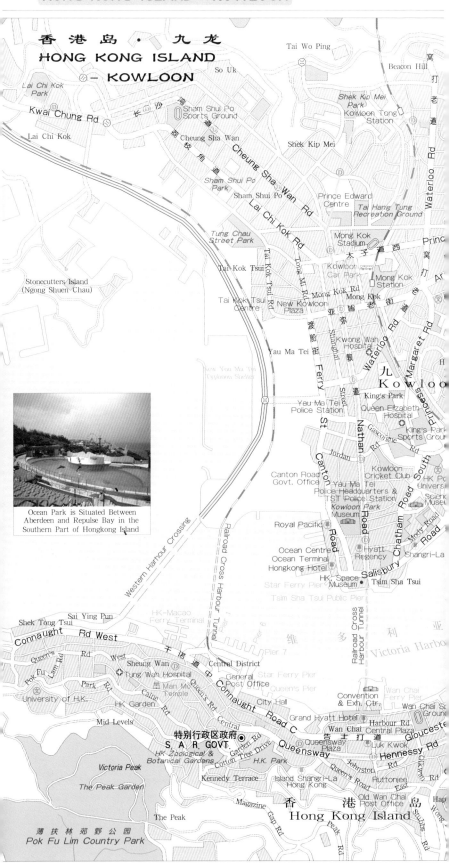

香港岛 · 九龙
HONG KONG ISLAND
— KOWLOON

Tai Wo Ping

Beacon Hill

窝
打
老
道

So Uk

Lai Chi Kok
Park

Sham Shui Po
Sports Ground

Shek Kip Mei
Park
Kowloon Tong
Station

Kwai Chung Rd

Cheung Sha Wan

Shek Kip Mei

Lai Chi Kok

长 沙

Sham Shui Po
Park

Prince Edward
Centre

Tai Hang Tung
Recreation Ground

窝
打
老
道

Sham Shui Po

Cheung Sha Wan Rd

Tung Chau
Street Park

Mong Kok
Stadium

太 子 道 西

Prince

Stonecutters Island
(Ngong Shuen Chau)

Tai Kok Tsui

Lai Chi Kok Rd

Tai Kok Tsui Rd

Tong Mi Rd

Kowloon
Car Park

Mong Kok
Station

打

Ar

Tai Kok Tsui
Centre

New Kowloon
Plaza

Mong Kok Rd

Mong Kok

亚 皆 老 街

街

Shanghai

Yau Ma Tei 街

Kwong Wah
Hospital

Waterloo Rd

Margaret Rd

九
Kowloo

New You Ma Tei
Typhoon Shelter

Ferry

Street

King's Park

Queen Elizabeth
Hospital

King's Park
Sports Grou

H

Yau Ma Tei
Police Station

渡
船
道

Gascoigne
Rd

Canton
St

Jordan
Rd

Kowloon
Cricket Club

HK Po
Universi

Canton Road
Govt. Office

Yau Ma Tei
Police Headquarters &
TST Police Station

Kowloon Park
Museum

Mody Road

Scienc
Musei

Royal Pacific

Road

Ocean Centre
Ocean Terminal
Hongkong Hotel

Hyatt
Regency

Nathan Road

Salisbury Chatham

Shangri-la

Road

Road

HK. Space
Museum

Tsim Sha Tsui

Star Ferry Pier

Tsim Sha Tsui Public Pier

Railroad Cross Harbour Tunnel

Victoria Harbo

维

多

利

亚

Sai Ying Pun

Shek Tong Tsui

HK-Macao
Ferry Terminal

Pier 7

Connaught Rd West

West

Sheung Wan
Tung Wah Hospital

Central District

Star Ferry Pier

Queen's Pier

Wan Chai Ferry Pier

Wan Chai St
Ground

Queen's Rd

Pok Fu Lam Rd

Rd

Caine Rd

Queen's Rd Central

Man Mo
Temple

HK Garden

Park Rd

University of H.K.

Mid Levels

Connaught Road C

General
Post Office

City Hall

Queensway

Grand Hyatt Hotel

Convention
& Exh. Ctr.

告 士 打 道

Wan Chai

Wan Chai Central Plaza

Harbour Rd

Gloucests

Luk Kwok

Hennessy Rd

O'Brien Rd

特别行政区政府
S. A. R. GOVT.

HK. Zoological &
Botanical Gardens

Cotton Tree Drive

Garden Rd

Queensway
Plaza

H.K. Park

Johnston Rd

Queen's Road

Puttonjee

Rd

East

Victoria Peak

The Peak Garden

Kennedy Terrace

Island Shangri-La
Hong Kong

香

港

岛

Old Wan Chai
Post Office

Hong Wong St

Hap

Magazine

Gap Rd

The Peak

Peak Rd

Stubbs Rd

Hong Kong Island

薄 扶 林 郊 野 公 园
Pok Fu Lim Country Park

Western Harbour Crossing

Railroad Cross Harbour Tunnel

Ocean Park is Situated Between
Aberdeen and Repulse Bay in the
Southern Part of Hongkong Island

Diamond Hill

Ngau Tei Wan

Wong Tai Sin Temple

g Tau Hom

Wong Tai Sin

Wong Tai Hom
Police Station

ong

San Po Kong

hai

Kowloon City

Kowloon City
Plaza

Prince Edward Rd E

d W

Ngau Chi Wan

Tian Tan Buddha Is Standing
on the top of Lantau Peak

Jorgan Valley

Kowloon
Sports Centre

Sung Wong
Toi Park

Wai

Sung Wong
Toi Road

Ma Tau Wai Rd

Kowloon City Rd

To To Kwa Wan

Kowloon City
Ferry Pier

Ngau Tau Kok
Police Station

Kowloon Wan

Ngau Tau Kok

KwunTong Road

Sau Mau Ping
Police Station

Ngau Tau Kok Rd

Kok Rd

North

Ma Tau Wai Rd

Hung Hom
Plaza

Ma Govt.
Building

Hung Hom
Whampoa
Garden

Kowloon City
Ferry Pier

Kowloon Bay

Kwun Tong
Typhoon Shelter

Kwun Tong

East Kowloon
Plaza

Kwun Tong
Industry Centre

Kwun Tong

Kwun Tong
Ferry Pier

Tin Hau Temple

Cha Kwo Ling

Cha Kwo Ling

on

Hung Hom Ferry Pier

Eastern Harbour Crossing

Railroad Cross Harbour Tunnel

North Point Ferry Pier

走
Java
廊
Rd

City Garden

Electric
Rd

皇
道

King's

Island
Eastern Corridor

Rd

Quarry Bay

ay Bay

North Point
Centre

North Point

Tai Koo Shing

Sai Wan Ho
Ferry Pier

东

Choi Sai Woo Park

Sai Wan Ho

维多利亚公园
ctoria Park
ade

Tin Hau Temple

Shau Kei Wan
Police Station

Shau Kei Wan Rd

ay Bay

Causeway Rd

Tai Hang

New Cathay

Shau Kei Wan

Tai Hang Rd

aroline Hill

Tung Wah Hospital

Aw Boon Haw Gardens

Hong Kong
Stadium

大 潭 郊 野 公 园
Tai Tam Country Park

Located to the east of the Zhujiang River estuary, Hongkong S.A.
adjoins Shenzhen on the north and faces the Nanhai Sea(South China Sea).
consists of Hongkong Island, Kowloon Peninsula, New Territories and the
small islands it governs and the sea areas. Area: 1095 km².

Since ancient times, Hongkong has been an inalienable part of the te
ritory of China. It was occupied by UK after the Opium War in 1840. Ac
ording to the Sino-British Joint Declaration on December 19, 1984, Ch
resumed the exercise of sovereignty over Hongkong on July 1, 1997 and founded Hongko
Special Administrative Region.

Scale 1:300000

0   3   6   9 km

Chengtouzui

Shitoujiao

Shatoujiao

Ap Chau   Crooked Island

Lin Ma Hang   Sai O

Yung Shue Au

Nanjao

廣

GUANGDONG

Ping Chau

Crescent Island

Lai Chi Wo

Luk Keng   Mui Tsz Lam

Nam Chung

Koki Tung

Wu Kau Tang   Sam A Chung

Double Island

东

Hok Tau Wai

Hung Shek Mun Tsuen

Egong

八仙岭郊野公园

t Sin Leng Country Park

Prot Island

大 鹏 湾
Dapeng Wan
(Mirs Bay)

Tai Mei Tuk

Grass Island

Tap Mun

Daih Wan

Shueh Wan

Hoi Ha

Sha Lan

Lai Chi Chong

Ma Shi Chau

Pak Sha

Tan Ka Wan

Pak Sha O

Tolo Harbour

Wu Kai Sha

Yung Shue O

Sai O

Chek Keng

Ma Liu Shui

Ma On Shan

西贡西郊野公园

Tun Ha

Sai Kung West Country Park

Ham Tin   Tai Long Tsui

ese University

Tai Shui Hang

Wong Chuk Wan

Tsak Yue Wu

Chuk Yeung

Lung Mei

Tai Mong Tsai

Sai Wan

Tai Long Wan

Po Tan

Sai Kung

Yim Tin Tsai   Yuen Ng Fan

Long Ke

Shatin

Wu Lei Tau

Pak Wai

Shaip
Island

Kau Sai Chau

High Island

Ho Chung

Nam Wai

Tung A

San Po Kong

Tai Po Tsai

Town Island

Jin Island

Wang Chau

Tseung Kwan O

Shelter Island

Basalt Island

Pan Long Wan

Pak Shing Kok

Bluff Island

Tai Hang Hau

North Point

Tai Wan Tau

Lei Yue Mun

Fat Tong Chau

Steep Island

Chai Wan

Siu Sai Wan

North Ninepin Island

Ninedin Group

大潭郊野公园

Nam Tong

South Ninepin Island

Tai Tam
Country Park

Tung Lung Chau

Chung Hom Cape

Shek O

南 海
Nan Hai
(South China Sea)

Chek Chue

Round
Island

Hok Tsui Wan

Cape D'Aguilar

Hongkong To Shanghai 825(1528)

Sung Kong

Beaufort Island

Waglan Island

Po Toi

Po Toi Islands

Hongkong To Kwangchow 39(120)

Hongkong occupies the extension of the hilly land   south of   Nanling ge and has a subtropical maritime climate. The annual mean temperature 2.8°C, and the annual average precipitation is 2225 mm.   Autumn is the season in a year. The main scenic spots include the History   Museum, anical Garden, Ocean Park and Taiping Hill(Victoria Peak), etc.   Besides, Tai O,   a town on tau Island reputed as the Venice of Hongkong, is also worth visiting.   It abounds in temples, Hau Temple is one of the most famous ones.

澳门半岛
MACAO PENINSULA

Ma Kwok Temple is situated in the south part of Macao Peninsula

ZHUHAI 珠海

广 DONG 东

S. Paulo Archway
is situated in the middl part
of Macao Peninsula

Friendship Bridge

外港 Outer Harbour

Man Wa Tung Fong

Macao Cultural Centre

Racing Vehicle Museum

Avenida

Kam Yue

Ho Hin Park

XIAN XING HAI A.

A. Paris

Rua de Governador Roma

Rua de J.S. Marques

Rua de Madrid

Cidade de Santarem

Sung Yue Sheng (Dr. Carlos) Park

Cidade de Coimbra

Rua de Braga

Statue of The Goddess of Mercy

Cidade de Sir Anders Ljungstedt

A. Marginal da Baía Nova

A. Dr. Sun Yat-Sen

A. Zheng Guan Ying

Rua de

Avenida de Sagres

Rua do Francisco

Estrada do Francisco

S. do Estrada de

Avenida

Guia Hill

Assembly Hall of Macao

Rua do Campo

Macao Daily

A. da Praia Grande

A. do Infante D. Henrique

Macao - Taipa Bridge

Man-made Lake

A. Dr. Maria Soares

S.A.R. GOVT. 特別行政区政府

Ma Rodrigues

International Hotel

A. de Almeida Ribeiro

Rua do Pedro António

Macao Hotel

Rua 2

Peninsula Hotel

Rua das Lorchas

Rua do Almirante Sérgio

Rua da Barra

Penha Cathadral & Bishop's Residence

Children's Park

Penha Hill

Ma Kwok Temple (Da Barra)

Navy Museum

Govt. Dock

Governor's Residence

Avenida da República

Ma Kwok Hill

Santiago Hotel

民国大马路

Man-made Lake

Inner Harbour

内港

澳门特别行政区 MACAO SPECIAL ADMINISTRATIVE REGION

1:70000

Scale 0   0.7   1.4   2.1 km

ZHUHAI 珠海

Barrier Gate

Qianshan Channel

Nanbao
Shifaozui
Wanzai

Kun Iam Temple
Ma Kai
Tin Hai Temple
Temple of God of Earth
Reservoir

澳
门
半
岛
Macao Peninsula

S. Paulo Archway
(The Remaining Facade
of St. Paul's Basilica)

91 ▲ Guia Hill

澳门
MACAO

Ma Wok Temple
(Pagode Da Barra)

Ho Hin Park

Sung Yue Sheng
(Dr. Carlos) Park

Statue of The
Goddess of Mercy

Inner Harbour

Macao-Taipa Bridge

Friendship Bridge

Zhujiang Kou 珠江口

广 东 GUANGDONG

Yanghuan

Grand Relief
Sculpture

Kun Iam Temple

112

Siu Tam Hill ▲

Pipal Garden

Macao University

凼 仔 岛
Taipa Island

160
Tai Tam Hill ▲

⊕ Macao International Airport

Horse-Racing Course

Macao Stadium

Runway

Xiacun

Hengqin

Lianhua Bridge

Zhongxin Gou

Ka Ho Bay
Ka Ho Deepwater
Fuel Wharf

Seac Pai Van
Pond

Ka Ho Res.
Ka Ho
Ka Ho Hill
▲ 132

Shishancun

Seac Pai Van
Country Park

路 环 岛
Coloane Island

Cushahuan

Museum of Land
& Nature History

Statue of A-Ma

Hac Sa Bay

Huoshao Shan
101 ▲

Tap Seac Tong Hill
▲ 172

Hac Sa
Hac Sa Park

Hengqin Economic
Development Area

S. Francisco Cathedral

Cheo Van Barbecue Park

Tam Kong Temple

Cheo Van Seaside

Cheo Van Bay

Situated to the west of the Zhujiang River estuary and standing opposite Hongkong , Macao comprises a small , narrow peninsula projecting from Guangdong Province and the islands of Taipa and Coloane. Area: 23.5 km².

Macao has been an inalienable part of the territory of China since ancient times, and was occupied by portugal after the Opium War. According to the Sino–Portuguese joint Declaration on April 13, 1987, China resumed the exercise of sovereignty over Macao and founded Macao Special Administrative Region on December 20, 1999.

Macao peninsula and the islands consist of some small granite hills, with limited areas of flatland. The highest point is on the Coloane Island. There are no permanent rivers in Macao.

Macao enjoys a subtropic maritime monsoon climate. It has a hot and humid summer, but a delightful winter. The annual mean temperature is 22.3°C. Four--fifths of Macao's annual rainfall falls within the summer rainy season. The annual average preciptation is 2031 mm.

The main scenic spots include Pagode Da Barra, S. Paulo Archway, Grand Fort, Pipal Garden, famous Black Sand Beach, Macao Museum, etc.

88
89

TAIPEI

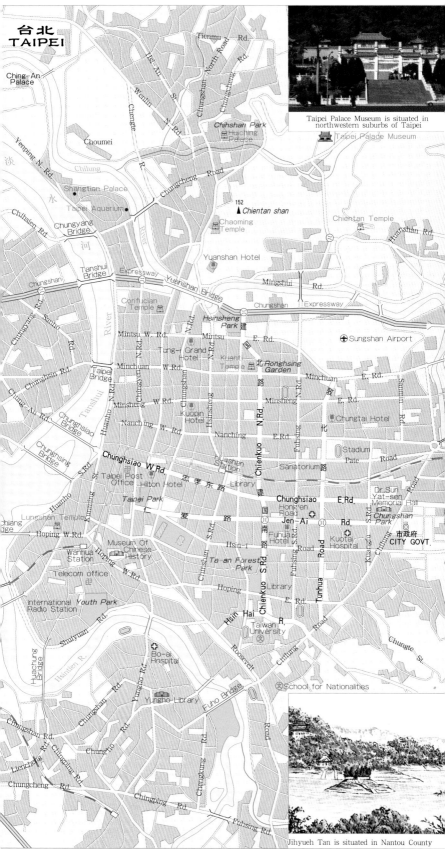

台北
TAIPEI

Ching-An
Palace

Choumei

Shangtian Palace

Taipei Aquarium

Chungyang
Bridge

Chihsten Rd

Yenping N. Rd.

Chilung

Tsi-An St.

Wenlin

Chengte

N. Rd.

Chungshan North Road

Chungcheng

Tienmu Rd.

Rd.

Chihshan Park
Huiching
Palace

152 ▲ Chientan shan

Chaoming
Temple

Yuanshan Hotel

Taipei Palace Museum is situated in
northwestern suburbs of Taipei

Taipei Palace Museum

Chientan Temple

Huanshan Rd.

Mingshui Rd.

Chungshan Expressway

Sungshan Airport

Tanshui
Bridge

Chungshan

Expressway

Yuanshan Bridge

Confucian
Temple

Mintsu W. Rd.

Tung-I
Grand
Hotel

Minchuan
W. Rd.

Minsheng W. Rd.

Nanching W. Rd.

Mintsu E. Rd.

Kuant
Temple 北

Ronghsing
Garden

Minsheng

Minchuan E. Rd.

E. Rd.

Chungtai Hotel

Samin Rd.

Chungshin Rd.

Ching-An Rd.

Chunghsiao
Bridge

Chungsing
Bridge

Kuopin
Hotel

Nanching

Hwashan
Station

Chienkuo

E. Rd.

化

Sanho Rd.

Huanho N.Rd.

Hsinsheng

Fuhsing N. Rd.

E. Rd.

Stadium

Sanatorium

Pate Road

Chunghsiao W. Rd.

Taipei Post
Office

Hilton Hotel

Library

建

Chunghsiao E. Rd.

Hong'en
Road

Jen-Ai Rd.

Dr. Sun
Yat-sen
Memorial Hall

Chungshan
Park

市政府
CITY GOVT.

Lungshan Temple

Hoping W. Rd.

Wanhua
Station

Museum Of
Chinese
History

Telecom office

Hsin-i

Fuhua
Hotel

Kuotai
Hospital

Road

Kuangfu

Chilung

International
Radio Station

Youth Park

Ta-an Forest
Park

Hoping

Chienkuo S. Rd.

Library

Tunhua

Bo-ai
Hospital

Hsin Hai R.

Taiwan
University

E. Rd.

Chungte St.

School for Nationalities

Yungho Library

Fuho Bridge

Chungshan Rd.

Chungho

Chingchang Rd.

Roosevelt

Chilung

Chengtung Rd.

Liencheng Rd.

Chungcheng Rd.

Chingping Rd.

Fuhsing Rd.

Jihyueh Tan is situated in Nantou County

147

Situated in a sea area off the southeast of China's mainland, facing Fuji
Province across the Taiwan Strait, and the Philippines across the Bashi Cha
nel, Taiwan Province consists of Taiwan Island and other islands, and
surrounding sea areas. Area:36000 km².

Taiwan Island is the largest in China. It is dominated by mountainous
hilly areas which occupy 2/3 of its total land. Mts.Yushan, known as " t
Roof of the Treasured Island,"is the highest mountain in the province,with
elevation of 3997 metres above sea level. The terraced tablelands and allu
plains are found along the western part of the island.

Because of the Tropic of Cancer passing through the province, it enjoys a tropic and s

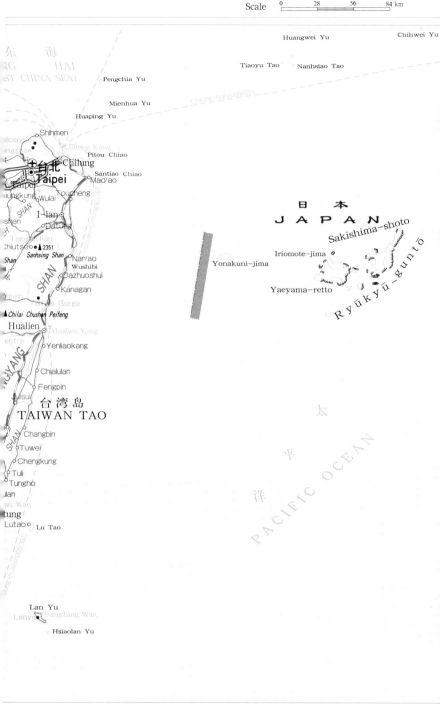

東　海
ONG　HAI
ST CHINA SEA)

Huangwei Yu

Chihwei Yu

Tiaoyu Tao   Nanhsiao Tao

Pengchia Yu

Mienhua Yu

Huaping Yu

olcano
ngshan
Shihmen

Chilung Kang
Pitou Chiao

Chilung

Santiao Chiao
Mao'ao

台北
Taipei
aipei

ungkung
Wulai
Toucheng

SHAN
I-lan
aTung

shan

Taipingshan
hiutse
2351
Sanhsing Shan
Nan'ao
Wushibi

Shan
Dazhuoshui

huan
Kanagan

nu Gorge

Chilai Chushan Peifeng

Hualien

Hualien Kang

entre
Yenliaokang

UYANG
Chialulan

Ju'sui
Fengpin

台湾岛
TAIWAN TAO

SHAN
Changbin

Tuwei

Chengkung

Tuli

Tungho
ulan

an Wan

ung

Lutao
Lu Tao

日　本
J A P A N

Sakishima-shoto

Iriomote-jima

Yonakuni-jima

Ryūkyū-guntō

Yaeyama-retto

太

平

洋

PACIFIC OCEAN

Lan Yu
Lanyu
Tungching Wan

Hsiaolan Yu

c climate characterized by the hot,rainy and windy weather.The annual
temperature is 22°C and the annual precipitation is more than 2400 mm.
aiwan has been an inalienable part of China's territory since ancient
s,which is an indisputable fact.

aiwan Province has rich tourist resources,with beautiful scenery of green
and clear waters,and has been known as "the Beautiful Treasured Island." The major scenic
s include Jihyuehtan Lake, Alishan Scenic Area, Mt.Yushan, Shihtou Hill, Temple of Cheng
ngkung(Zheng Chenggong), and the Palace Museum in Taipei, etc.

ecial local products include shell carving picture in Lutao,glassware in Taipei,art pottery and
elain in Peitou, etc. Nantou has the largest centre of butterfly specimen in the world.

64-65

CHINA'S MAJOR HOTELS　中国主要宾馆饭店

LOCATION	NAME & STARS　名称、星级	ADDRESS　地址	TELEPHONE 电
Beijing 北京 * 010	Kempinski Hotel Beijing Lufthansa Center ☆☆☆☆☆ 北京凯宾斯基饭店	50 Liangmaqiao Lu, Chaoyang District 朝阳区亮马桥路50号	64653388 64653366
	China World Hotel,Beijing ☆☆☆☆☆ 中国大饭店	1 Jianguomenwai Dajie,Dabeiyao. 大北窑建国门外大街1号	65052266 65050828
	The Great Wall Sheraton Hotel ☆☆☆☆☆ 北京长城饭店	10 Dongsanhuan Beilu, Chaoyang District 朝阳区东三环北路10号	65905566 65905938
	Kunlun Hotel ☆☆☆☆☆ 昆仑饭店	2 Xinyuan Nanlu 朝阳区新源南路2号	65903388 65903228
	New Century Hotel ☆☆☆☆☆ 新世纪饭店	6 Shoudutiyuguan Nanlu 海淀区首都体育馆南路6号	68492001 68491103
	Hotel New Otani Changfugong ☆☆☆☆☆ 长富宫饭店	26 Jianguomenwai Dajie 朝阳区建国门外大街26号	65125555 65139810
	Holiday Inn Crown Plaza ☆☆☆☆☆ 国际艺苑皇冠假日饭店	48 Wangfujing Dajie 东城区王府井大街48号	65133388 65132513
	Grand Hotel ☆☆☆☆☆ 贵宾楼饭店	35 Dongchang'an Jie 东城区东长安街35号	65137788 65130048
	Jingguang New World Hotel ☆☆☆☆☆ 京广新世纪饭店	Hujialou,Chaoyang District 朝阳区呼家楼路口	65978888 65973333
	Shangri-La Hotel ☆☆☆☆☆ 香格里拉饭店	29 Zizhuyuan Lu 海淀区紫竹院路29号	68412211 68418002
	Swissotel Beijing,Hong Kong Macao Center ☆☆☆☆☆ 港澳中心瑞士饭店	Dongsishitiao Lijiaoqiao 东城区东二环东四十条立交桥	65012288 65012501
	Prime Hotel ☆☆☆☆☆ 皇都酒店	2 Wangfujing Dajie 东城区王府井大街2号	65136666 65134248
	The Palace Hotel ☆☆☆☆☆ 王府饭店	8 Jinyuhutong, Dongdan Beidajie 东城区东单北大街金鱼胡同8号	65128899 65129050
	Beijing Hotel ☆☆☆☆☆ 北京饭店	33 Dongchang'an Jie 东城区东长安街33号	65137766 65137307
Tianjin 天津 022	Tianjin Sheraton Hotel ☆☆☆☆☆ 喜来登大酒店	Zijinshan Lu,Hexi District 河西区紫金山路	23343388 23358740
	Hyatt Tianjin ☆☆☆☆ 凯悦饭店	219 Jiefang Beilu 解放北路219号	23314222
	Astor Hotel ☆☆☆☆ 利顺德大饭店	33 Taierzhuang Lu 台儿庄路33号	23311688 23316282
	Crystal Palace Hotel ☆☆☆☆ 水晶宫饭店	Binshuidao, Youyi Lu, Hexi District 河西区友谊路、滨水道交口	28356666
	Geneva Hotel ☆☆☆☆ 津利华大酒店	32 Youyi Lu,Hexi District 河西区友谊路32号	28352222 28359855

LOCATION	NAME & STARS 名称、星级	ADDRESS 地址	TELEPHONE 电话
Shijiazhuang 石家庄 0311	Hebei Hotel ☆☆☆☆ 河北宾馆	168 Yucai Jie 育才街168号	5815961 5814092
Taiyuan 太原 0351	Yingze Hotel ☆☆☆☆ 迎泽饭店	189 Yingze Dajie 迎泽大街189号	4043211
Hohhot 呼和浩特 0471	Inner Mongolia Hotel ☆☆☆ 内蒙古饭店	31 Ulanqab Xilu 乌兰察布西路31号	6964233
	Xincheng Hotel ☆☆☆☆☆ 新城饭店	40 Hulun Nanlu 呼伦南路40号	6292288
Shenyang 沈阳 024	Liaoning Tiandu Hotel ☆☆☆ 辽宁天都饭店	238 Nanwu Malu,Heping District 和平区南五马路238号	23866939 23867615
	Liaoning Phoenix Hotel ☆☆☆ 辽宁凤凰饭店	109 Huanghe Nandajie 黄河南大街109号	86805858
Dalian 大连 0411	Holiday Inn ☆☆☆☆☆ 九洲假日饭店	18 Shengli Guangchang, Zhongshan District 中山区胜利广场18号	2808888
	Lijing Hotel ☆☆☆☆☆ 丽景大酒店	12 Hutan Jie,Zhongshan District 中山区虎滩街12号	2892811
	Furama Hotel ☆☆☆☆ 富丽华饭店	60 Renmin Lu 人民路60号	2630888
Changchun 长春 0431	Mingmen Hotel ☆☆☆☆☆ 名门宾馆	135 Renming Dajie 人民大街135号	5622888
	Shangri-La Hotel ☆☆☆☆☆ 香格里拉饭店	9 Xi'an Dajie 西安大路9号	8981818
	Changchun Guest House ☆☆☆ 长春宾馆	18 Xinhua Lu 新华路18号	8929920 8922033
Harbin 哈尔滨 0451	New World Beifang Hotel ☆☆☆☆ 新世纪北方酒店	403 Huayuan Jie,Nangang District 南岗区花园街403号	3628888 3622828
Shanghai 上海 021	Garden Hotel ☆☆☆☆☆ 花园饭店	58 Maoming Nanlu 茂名南路58号	64151234 64158866
	New Jinjiang Tower ☆☆☆☆☆ 新锦江饭店	161 Changle Lu 长乐路161号	64151188 64150048
	Portman-Shangrila Hotel ☆☆☆☆☆ 波特曼丽思卡尔顿酒店	1376 Nanjing Xilu 南京西路1376号	62798888 62798800
	Jc Mandarin ☆☆☆☆☆ 锦沧文华大酒店	1225 Nanjing Xilu 南京西路1225号	62791888 62791822
	Huating Hotel & Towers ☆☆☆☆☆ 华亭宾馆	1200 Caoxi Beilu 漕溪北路1200号	64391000 62550830
	The Western Tai Ping Yang ☆☆☆☆☆ 威斯汀太平洋大饭店	5 Zunyi Nanlu 遵义南路5号	62758888 62755420
	Jing'an Hilton Hotel ☆☆☆☆☆ 静安希尔顿饭店	250 Huashan Lu 华山路250号	62480000 62483848
Nanjing 南京 025	Zhongyang Hotel ☆☆☆☆☆ 中央大厦	200 Zhongshan Lu 中山路200号	3361888 3377228

LOCATION	NAME & STARS 名称、星级	ADDRESS 地址	TELEPHONE
Nanjing 南京 025	Jinling Hotel ☆☆☆☆☆ 金陵饭店	Xinjiekou 新街口	4711888 4711999
Suzhou 苏州 0512	Suzhou Hotel ☆☆☆☆ 苏州饭店	115 Shiquan Jie 十全街115号	5204646 5205191
	Astor Hotel ☆☆☆☆☆ 雅都饭店	156 Sanxiang Lu 三香路156号	8291888 8291838
Hangzhou 杭州 0571	Shangri-La Hotel ☆☆☆☆☆ 香格里拉饭店	Beishan Lu 北山路	7977951
	Dragon Hotel ☆☆☆☆ 黄龙饭店	Shuguang Lu 曙光路	5154488
	Wanghu Hotel ☆☆☆☆ 望湖宾馆	2 Huancheng Xilu 环城西路2号	7071024 7071350
	The River of Hangzhou Hotel ☆☆☆☆ 杭州之江饭店	180-200 Moganshan Lu 莫干山路188-200号	8066888
	Zhijiang Holiday Resort ☆☆☆ 之江度假村	South of Qiantangjiang Bridge 钱塘江大桥南岸	86696888
Ningbo 宁波 0574	Donggang Hotel ☆☆☆ 东港大酒店	52 Caihong Beilu 彩虹北路52号	7373188 7333646
	Xinyuan Guest House ☆☆☆ 新园宾馆	188 Jiefang Nanlu 解放南路188号	7321818 7294439
Hefei 合肥 0551	Overseas Chinese Hotel ☆☆☆ 华侨饭店	98 Changjiang Lu 长江路98号	2652221 2642861
	Anhui Hotel ☆☆☆ 安徽饭店	18 Meishan Lu 梅山路18号	2811818 2817583
Fuzhou 福州 0591	Xihu Hotel ☆☆☆☆ 西湖大酒店	158 Hubin Lu 湖滨路158号	7839888 7836585
	Hot Spring Hotel ☆☆☆☆ 温泉大酒店	218 Wusi Lu 五四路218号	7851818 7835150
	Fujian Foreian Trade Centre Hotel ☆☆☆☆ 福建外贸中心酒店	73 Wusi Lu 五四路73号	7523388 7550358
Nanchang 南昌 0791	Jiangxi Hotel ☆☆☆☆ 江西宾馆	368 Bayi Dadao 八一大道368号	6221133 6214126
Jinan 济南 0531	Shandong Guiyou Hotel ☆☆☆☆ 山东贵友大酒店	101 Yingxiongshan Lu 英雄山路101号	2980088 2980099
	Qilu Hotel ☆☆☆☆ 齐鲁饭店	8 Qianfoshan Lu 千佛山路8号	2966888 2967676
Qingdao 青岛 0532	Grand Regency Hotel ☆☆☆☆☆ 丽晶大酒店	1 Taiwan Lu 台湾路1号	5881818 5881888
	Haitian Hotel ☆☆☆☆ 海天大酒店	39 Zhanshan Dalu 湛山大路39号	3871888 3871777
	Huiquan Dynasty Hotel ☆☆☆☆ 汇泉王朝大酒店	9 Nanhai Lu 南海9号	2873366 2871122

LOCATION	NAME & STARS 名称、星级	ADDRESS 地址	TELEPHONE 电话
Qingdao 青岛 0532	Haijinghuayuan Hotel ☆☆☆☆ 海景花园大饭店	2 Zhanghua Lu 彰化路2号	5875777 5894031
	Dongfang Hotel ☆☆☆ 东方饭店	4 Daxue Lu 大学路4号	2865888 2861741
Zhengzhou 郑州 0371	Dukang Hotel ☆☆☆ 杜康大酒店	178 Tongbai Lu 桐柏路178号	7976888 7635371
	Tianyuan Hotel ☆☆☆ 田园酒店	51 1 Malu 一马路51号	6969898
Wuhan 武汉 027	Asia Hotel ☆☆☆☆ 亚洲大酒店	616 Jiefang Dadao 解放大道616号	83807777
Changsha 长沙 0731	Huatian Hotel ☆☆☆☆ 华天大酒店	16 Jiefang Donglu 解放东路16号	4442888 4442270
Guangzhou 广州 020	White Swan Hotel ☆☆☆☆☆ 白天鹅宾馆	1 Shamian Nanjie 沙面南街1号	81886968 81861188
	Garden Hotel ☆☆☆☆☆ 花园饭店	368 Huanshi Donglu 环市东路368号	83338989 83350467
	China Hotel ☆☆☆☆☆ 中国大酒店	Liuhua Lu 流花路	86666888 86677014
	Dongfang Hotel ☆☆☆☆☆ 东方宾馆	120 Liuhua Lu 流花路120号	86669900 86662775
	International Hotel ☆☆☆☆☆ 国际大酒店	339 Huanshi Donglu 环市东路339号	83311888 83311666
Shenzhen 深圳 0755	Sunshine Hotel ☆☆☆☆☆ 阳光酒店	1 Jiabin Lu 嘉宾路1号	2233888 2226719
	Nanhai Hotel ☆☆☆☆☆ 南海酒店	Shekou Industrial Zone 蛇口工业区	6692888 6692440
	Landmark Hotel ☆☆☆☆☆ 富苑酒店	2 Nanhu Lu 南湖路2号	2172288 2290473
	Shangri-La Hotel ☆☆☆☆☆ 香格里拉大酒店	East Side of Railway Station 建设路火车站东侧	2230888 2339878
	Fulin Hotel ☆☆☆☆☆ 富临大酒店	67 Heping Lu 和平路67号	5586333 5561732
	Junhao Hotel ☆☆☆☆☆ 骏豪酒店	Guanlanzhen 观澜镇	8020888 8011111
Shantou 汕头 0754	Golden Gulf Hotel ☆☆☆☆☆ 金海湾大酒店	Jinsha Donglu 金砂东路	8263263 8265163
Zhuhai 珠海 0756	Zhuhai Hotel ☆☆☆☆ 珠海宾馆	Jingshan Lu 景山路	3333718 3332339
	Holiday Resort Hotel ☆☆☆☆ 度假村酒店	Shihuashan 石花山	3332038 3332036
Nanning 南宁 0771	Mingyuanxindu Hotel ☆☆☆☆☆ 明园新都饭店	38 Xinmin Lu 新民路38号	2830808

LOCATION	NAME & STARS 名称、星级	ADDRESS 地址	TELEPHONE
Nanning 南宁 0771	Yongjiang Hotel ☆☆☆☆ 甬江饭店	41 Jiangbin Donglu 江滨东路41号	2808123
	Jinyue Guest House ☆☆☆ 金悦宾馆	59 Xinmin Lu 新民路59号	2802338 2802450
Guilin 桂林 0773	Daewoo Hotel ☆☆☆☆☆ 大宇大饭店	Binjiang Nanlu 滨江南路	2825588 2825598
	Royal Garden Hotel ☆☆☆☆☆ 帝苑酒店	Yanjiang Lu 沿江路	5812411 5815051
Haikou 海口 0898	Golden Coast Luodun Hotel ☆☆☆☆☆ 金海岸罗顿大酒店	Renmin Lu,Haidiandao 海甸岛人民大道	6259888 6258889
	Huandao Taide Hotel ☆☆☆☆☆ 环岛泰得大酒店	Heping Lu,Haidiandao 海甸岛和平大道	6268888 6265588
Chongqing 重庆 023	Wanghao Hotel ☆☆☆☆☆ 望豪酒店	77 Qingnian Lu 青年路77号	63888888
	Yangtze River Holiday Hotel ☆☆☆☆ 扬子江假日饭店	15 Nanping Beilu 南坪北路15号	62803380 62800884
	Chongqing Guest House ☆☆☆☆ 重庆宾馆	235 Minsheng Lu 民生路235号	63845888 63830643
Chengdu 成都 028	Jinjiang Hotel ☆☆☆☆☆ 锦江宾馆	80. 2 Duan, Renmin Lu 人民南路二段80号	5582222 5582348
	Minshan Hotel ☆☆☆☆ 岷山饭店	55 2 Duan, Renmin Nanlu 人民南路二段55号	5585333
	Chengdu Hotel ☆☆☆☆ 成都饭店	Shudu Dadao 蜀都大道东段	4448888
Guiyang 贵阳 0851	Guizhou Hotel ☆☆☆ 贵州饭店	66 Beijing Lu 北京路66号	6822888 6824397
Kunming 昆明 0871	Jiahuaguangchang Hotel ☆☆☆☆☆ 佳华广场酒店	157 Beijing Lu 北京路157号	3562828
	Bangke Hotel ☆☆☆☆☆ 邦克饭店	399 Qingnian Lu 青年路399号	3158888
Lhasa 拉萨 0891	Holiday Inn Lahasa ☆☆☆ 假日饭店	1 Minzu Lu,850001,China 民族路1号	6832221
	Tibet Hotel ☆☆☆ 西藏宾馆	221 Beijing Xilu 北京西路221号	6834966
Xi'an 西安 029	Grand Castle Hotel Xi'an ☆☆☆☆☆ 长安城堡大酒店	12 Huangcheng Nanlu 环城南路西段12号	7231800 7231500
	Hyatt Xi'an ☆☆☆☆☆ 西安凯悦饭店	158 Dong Dajie 东大街158号	7231234 7216799
	Shangri-La Jinhua Hotel ☆☆☆☆☆ 香格里拉大饭店	8 Changle Xilu 长乐西路8号	3232981 3235477
	Sheraton Hotel ☆☆☆☆☆ 喜来登大酒店	12 Fenghao Lu 丰镐路12号	4261888 4262188

LOCATION	NAME & STARS 名称、星级	ADDRESS 地址	TELEPHONE 电话
Lanzhou 兰州 0931	Friendship Hotel ☆☆☆☆ 友谊饭店	16 Xijin Xilu 西津西路16号	2333051 2330304
	Lanzhou Hotel ☆☆☆ 兰州饭店	434 Donggang Xilu 东岗西路434号	8416321 8418608
	Jincheng Hotel ☆☆☆ 金城饭店	363 Tianshui Lu 天水路363号	8416638 6418438
	Feitian Hotel ☆☆☆ 飞天宾馆	599 Tianshui Lu 天水路599号	8882876
Xining 西宁 0971	Qinghai Hotel ☆☆☆ 青海饭店	158 Huanghe Lu 黄河路158号	6144888 6144145
	Xining Hotel ☆☆☆ 西宁饭店	348 Qiyi Lu 七一路348号	8238701 8238798
Yinchuan 银川 0951	International Hotel ☆☆☆ 国际饭店	25 Beihuan Donglu 北环东路25号	6728688 6711808
Ürümqi 乌鲁木齐 0991	Holiday Inn ☆☆☆☆ 新疆假日大饭店	168 Xinhua Beilu 新华北路168号	2818788
	World Plaza Hotel ☆☆☆☆ 新疆环球大酒店	2 Beijing Nanlu 北京南路2号	3836360 3836399

* The number under a city indicates the city's area corde (telephone).

APPENDIX 2

TELEPHONE NUMBERS OF COMMON USE

中国国际字冠	China Int'l code	0086
电话查号台	Tel Inquiry	114
旅游热线电话（北京）	Tourist Hot Line (Beijing)	65130858
急救电话	First Aid	120
报警电话	Police	110
火警电话	Fire	119
天气预报台	Weather Forecast	121
报时台	Time Report	117

INDEX OF CHINA'S PRINCIPAL CITIES

Songyuan	松原	40	Xuchang	许昌	79	
Suihua	绥化	45	Xuzhou	徐州	52	
Suining	遂宁	105	Yaan	雅安	104	
Suizhou	随州	81	Yan'an	延安	124	
Suqian	宿迁	52	Yancheng	盐城	53	
Suzhou	苏州	50、52	Yangjiang	阳江	88	
Suzhou	宿州	60	Yangquan	阳泉	28	
Tai'an	泰安	72	Yangzhou	扬州	50、53	
Taipei	台北	147、149	Yantai	烟台	73	
Taiyuan	太原	28、30	Yibin	宜宾	105	
Taizhou	台州	57	Yichang	宜昌	80	
Taizhou	泰州	53	Yichun	伊春	45	
Tangshan	唐山	24	Yichun	宜春	68	
Tianjin	天津	21、22−23	Yinchuan	银川	135、136	
Tianshui	天水	129	Yingkou	营口	37	
Tieling	铁岭	37	Yingtan	鹰潭	68	
Tongchuan	铜川	125	Yiyang	益阳	84	
Tonghua	通化	40	Yongzhou	永州	85	
Tongliao	通辽	33	Yueyang	岳阳	84	
Tongling	铜陵	61	Yulin	榆林	124	
Ürümqi	乌鲁木齐	137、139	Yulin	玉林	93	
Weifang	潍坊	73	Yuncheng	运城	29	
Weihai	威海	73	Yunfu	云浮	88	
Weinan	渭南	125	Yuxi	玉溪	117	
Wenzhou	温州	57	Zaozhuang	枣庄	72	
Wuhai	乌海	32	Zhangjiajie	张家界	84	
Wuhan	武汉	81、82	Zhangjiakou	张家口	24	
Wuhu	芜湖	61	Zhangzhou	漳州	65	
Wuxi	无锡	51、53	Zhanjiang	湛江	88	
Wuzhong	吴忠	136	Zhaoqing	肇庆	88	
Wuzhou	梧州	93	Zhaotong	昭通	117	
Xi'an	西安	125、126	Zhengzhou	郑州	77、79	
Xiamen	厦门	65、67	Zhenjiang	镇江	53	
Xiangfan	襄樊	80	Zhongshan	中山	88	
Xiangtan	湘潭	84	Zhoukou	周口	79	
Xianning	咸宁	81	Zhoushan	舟山	57	
Xianyang	咸阳	125	Zhuhai	珠海	88、90	
Xiaogan	孝感	81	Zhumadian	驻马店	79	
Xingtai	邢台	25	Zhuzhou	株洲	84	
Xining	西宁	133、134	Zibo	淄博	72	
Xinxiang	新乡	79	Zigong	自贡	105	
Xinyang	信阳	79	Ziyang	资阳	105	
Xinyu	新余	68	Zunyi	遵义	112	
Xinzhou	忻州	28	Guyuan	固原	136	
Xuancheng	宣城	61	Wuwei	武威	129	

WORLD NATURAL & CULTURAL HERITAGES IN CHINA
INDEX OF CHINA'S NATIONAL MAJOR FAMOUS SCENIC SPOTS

JS(2003)01—154

Designer:	Ma Guiju
Editors:	Zhao Jianjian Jiang Yonglin Fan Guoying
	Yuan Baoqing Zhao Erping Sui Yuxiu
	Liu Junqing Meng Jing
Compilers:	Fengjing Zong Chuanmeng Yao Xuehua
	Wangying Yuan Huining
	Xu Fenghua Xu Huining Chenglei
	Lai Xiaoyun Shi Kenong Sun Jianbo
	Liu Haizhen Tian Weibo Cao Deyi
	Chenjing
Checkers:	Wang Xiuzhi Kong Guangzheng Guo Lanling
	Fan Chengxiao Wang Jingyu Wang Yu
	Li Shufang Wu Tangxing
Translator:	Wang Liyi
Proofreader:	Wang Qichang
Examiner:	Du Zhiping

ISBN 7-80104-510-6

9 787801 045102 >

ISBN 7-80104-510-6/K · 367

Price: 36.00 Yuan